American Language Hub

CB127930

LEVEL 1B
Student's Book

PETER MAGGS
CATHERINE SMITH

macmillan education

Contents

Contents

Irregular Verbs

Infinitive	Past simple	Past participle
be	was/were	been
become	became	become
begin	began	begun
break	broke	broken
bring	brought	brought
build	built	built
buy	bought	bought
can	could	(been able to)
catch	caught	caught
choose	chose	chosen
come	came	come
cost	cost	cost
cut	cut	cut
do	did	done
drink	drank	drunk
eat	ate	eaten
fall	fell	fallen
feel	felt	felt
find	found	found
forget	forgot	forgotten
get	got	got
give	gave	given
go	went	gone/been
grow	grew	grown
have	had	had
hear	heard	heard
hit	hit	hit
hold	held	held
hurt	hurt	hurt
keep	kept	kept
know	knew	known
leave	left	left
lend	lent	lent

Infinitive	Past simple	Past participle
let	let	let
lose	lost	lost
make	made	made
mean	meant	meant
meet	met	met
must	had to	(had to)
pay	paid	paid
put	put	put
read	read	read
ride	rode	ridden
run	ran	run
say	said	said
see	saw	seen
sell	sold	sold
set	set	set
shut	shut	shut
sing	sang	sung
sit	sat	sat
sleep	slept	slept
speak	spoke	spoken
spell	spelled	spelled
spend	spent	spent
stand	stood	stood
steal	stole	stolen
take	took	taken
teach	taught	taught
tell	told	told
think	thought	thought
throw	threw	thrown
understand	understood	understood
wear	wore	worn
win	won	won
write	wrote	written

PHONETIC SYMBOLS

Single vowels			Diphthongs			Consonants					
/ɪ/	fi**sh**	/fɪʃ/	/ɪə/	**ear**	/ɪə/	/p/	**p**en	/pen/	/s/	**s**nake	/sneɪk/
/iː/	b**ea**n	/biːn/	/eɪ/	f**a**ce	/feɪs/	/b/	**b**ag	/bæg/	/z/	**z**oo	/zuː/
/ʊ/	f**oo**t	/fʊt/	/ʊə/	**tour**ist	/ˈtʊərɪst/	/t/	**t**ea	/tiː/	/ʃ/	**sh**op	/ʃɒp/
/uː/	sh**oe**	/ʃuː/	/ɔɪ/	b**oy**	/bɔɪ/	/d/	**d**og	/dɒg/	/ʒ/	televi**si**on	/ˈtelɪvɪʒən/
/e/	**e**gg	/eg/	/əʊ/	n**o**se	/nəʊz/	/tʃ/	**ch**ip	/tʃɪp/	/m/	**m**ap	/mæp/
/ə/	moth**er**	/ˈmʌðə/	/ju/	**u**se	/juz/	/dʒ/	**j**azz	/dʒæz/	/n/	**n**ame	/neɪm/
/ɜː/	w**or**d	/wɜːd/	/aɪ/	**eye**	/aɪ/	/k/	**c**ake	/keɪk/	/ŋ/	ri**ng**	/rɪŋ/
/ɔː/	t**al**k	/tɔːk/	/aʊ/	m**ou**th	/maʊθ/	/g/	**g**irl	/gɜːl/	/h/	**h**ouse	/haʊs/
/æ/	b**a**ck	/bæk/				/f/	**f**ilm	/fɪlm/	/l/	**l**eg	/leg/
/ʌ/	b**u**s	/bʌs/				/v/	**v**erb	/vɜːb/	/r/	**r**oad	/rəʊd/
/ɑː/	**ar**m	/ɑːm/				/θ/	**th**ing	/θɪŋ/	/w/	**w**ant	/wɒnt/
/ɒ/	t**o**p	/tɒp/				/ð/	**th**ese	/ðiːz/	/j/	**y**es	/jes/

7

TRAVEL AND TRANSPORTATION

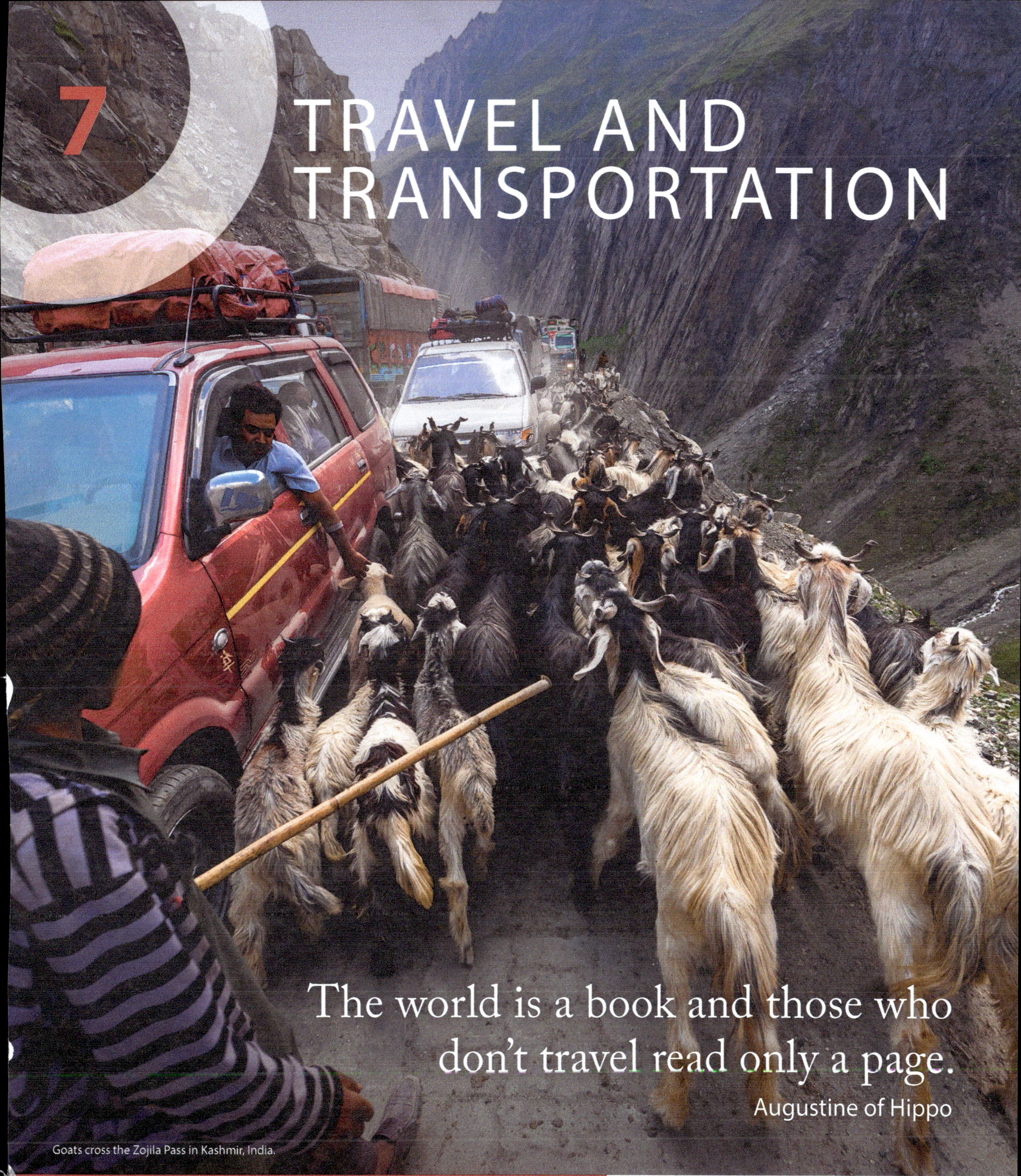

The world is a book and those who don't travel read only a page.

Augustine of Hippo

Goats cross the Zojila Pass in Kashmir, India.

OBJECTIVES

- talk about transportation in a city
- talk about a journey
- talk about a vacation
- check in and out of a hotel
- write a short article about a travel experience

Work with a partner. Discuss the questions.

1 Where did you go on vacation last year?
2 Look at the picture. Would you like to drive here? Why/Why not?
3 Which countries would you like to visit?

7.1 Getting around

Talk about transportation in a city

V transportation **P** /eɪ/ and /oʊ/ **G** *could*

VOCABULARY
Transportation

A Look at the pictures in *Where in the world are they?* What types of transportation can you see? What other types of transportation can you think of?

B Go to the **Vocabulary Hub** on **page XVIII**.

C SPEAK Work in pairs. Think about a time you were in a different country or city. Answer the questions.

1 What types of transportation did you use?
2 Were they difficult to use? Why?
3 Were they cheap or expensive?

When I was in Vietnam last year, I took a motorcycle taxi. It was cheap and easy to organize.

PRONUNCIATION
/eɪ/ and /oʊ/

7.1 **A** Listen and repeat the transportation words in the box.

boat coach motorcycle plane train

7.2 **B** Listen to the vowel sound /oʊ/ in boat. Then underline the words in the box in Exercise A that have the same vowel sound. What letters can make the /oʊ/ sound?

7.3 **C** Listen to the vowel sound /eɪ/ in plane. Then circle the words in the box in Exercise A that have the same vowel sound. What letters can make the /eɪ/ sound?

D SPEAK Work in pairs. Practice saying the transportation words. Listen and check your partner's pronunciation. Be careful to pronounce the words correctly.

READING

A READ FOR GIST Read *Where in the world are they?* What is it about?

1 buildings 2 countries 3 transportation

B SPEAK Work in pairs. Complete the quiz.

C SCAN Read *Six quick facts*. Match facts (a–f) with pictures (1–6) in the quiz.

D READ FOR DETAIL Read *Six quick facts* again. Answer the questions.

1 How old are the buses in Mumbai? ________
2 How many San Francisco trolleys are there today? ________
3 How many subway stations are there in Moscow? ________
4 What two types of transportation can you take from Amsterdam station? ________
5 Where does the Star Ferry go between? ________
6 What are three popular types of transportation in Hanoi? ________

E SPEAK Work in pairs. Think about the cities in the quiz. Which do you think are difficult to travel around? Why?

A: I think it's easy to travel around Hong Kong. It's a fairly small place. What do you think?
B: Yes, I agree.

Where in the world are they?

Do you know what color the taxis are in New York? And which Italian city has no cars? If you answered *yellow* and *Venice*, take our quiz!

Look at the pictures 1–6. Where are they? Choose a, b, or c.

1 a Mumbai b Hong Kong c London
2 a Lisbon b San Francisco c Mexico City
3 a Hanoi b Bangkok c Manila
4 a Budapest b Moscow c Kiev
5 a Shanghai b Sydney c Hong Kong
6 a Berlin b Amsterdam c Rio de Janeiro

Answers: 1 a, 2 b, 3 a, 4 b, 5 c, 6 b

GRAMMAR
could

A WORK IT OUT Scan *Six quick facts* again. Underline sentences with *could* or *couldn't*.

B Look at the sentences you underlined in Exercise A and complete the rules.

could
1 We use *could* to talk about abilities in the ***past* / *present***.
2 We use *could* ***before* / *after*** the main verb.
3 We use the ***infinitive* / *base form*** after *could*.
4 The ***negative* / *future*** form of *could* is *couldn't*.

C Go to the **Grammar Hub** on **page VI**.

D SPEAK Work in pairs. Tell your partner some things you *could* and *couldn't* do or see five or ten years ago.

A: Five years ago, I couldn't drive a car.
B: Ten years ago, you could see a lot of bicycles in my town.

SPEAKING

A PREPARE Think about the transportation in a city you know well.

B Write some questions to ask your partner about the transportation in their city. Use the ideas below to help you.

1 what / color / buses? *What color are the buses?*
2 is / river? ______
3 is / ferry? ______
4 where / ferry / go / between? ______
5 how many / train stations? ______
6 are / many / traffic jams? ______
7 bicycles / popular? ______

C SPEAK Work in pairs. Ask questions and guess your partner's city. Then answer questions about your city.

A: What color are the taxis?
B: They're yellow.
A: Is there a ferry?
B: Yes, there is.
A: Where does the ferry go between?
B: The main ferry goes between Queens and Manhattan.

Six quick facts

a ___ Scooters and motorcycles are the most common type of transportation in Hanoi, Vietnam. There are also lots of bicycles. Twenty years ago, you couldn't see so many scooters and motorcycles on Hanoi's streets, but you could see a lot of bicycles.

b ___ Every day, 250,000 people go through Amsterdam Central Station. It's the city's main train and bus station.

c ___ The famous Star Ferry in Hong Kong carries over 70,000 passengers a day between Hong Kong Island and Kowloon. That's 26 million passengers a year!

d ___ No, this isn't London – it's Mumbai! These Indian buses are 80 years old. The design and color is the same as London buses.

e ___ Take a trolley in San Francisco for a traditional experience. But there aren't many these days. One hundred years ago, you could see hundreds of trolleys in San Francisco. Today, there are only about 40.

f ___ Opened in 1935, there are now 206 subway stations in Moscow. Many of the stations are very beautiful. Each one is like an art gallery.

Talk about transportation in a city

G simple past negative   V travel phrases   P word stress: cities

READING

A Work in pairs. Look at the routes around the world. Which route would you take? Why?

B **READ FOR GIST** Read *The Nellie Bly route*. Which route in Exercise A matches the one Nellie Bly took?

TRADITIONAL TRAVEL ADVENTURES

We travel the traditional way: by boat, train and bus.

Route 1: London, Reykjavík, St. Petersburg, Tokyo, Sydney, Cape Town, Rio de Janeiro

Route 2: New York, London, Paris, Brindisi, Port Said, Singapore, Hong Kong, Tokyo, San Francisco

Route 3: Miami, Cancún, Lima, Melbourne, Nairobi, Munich

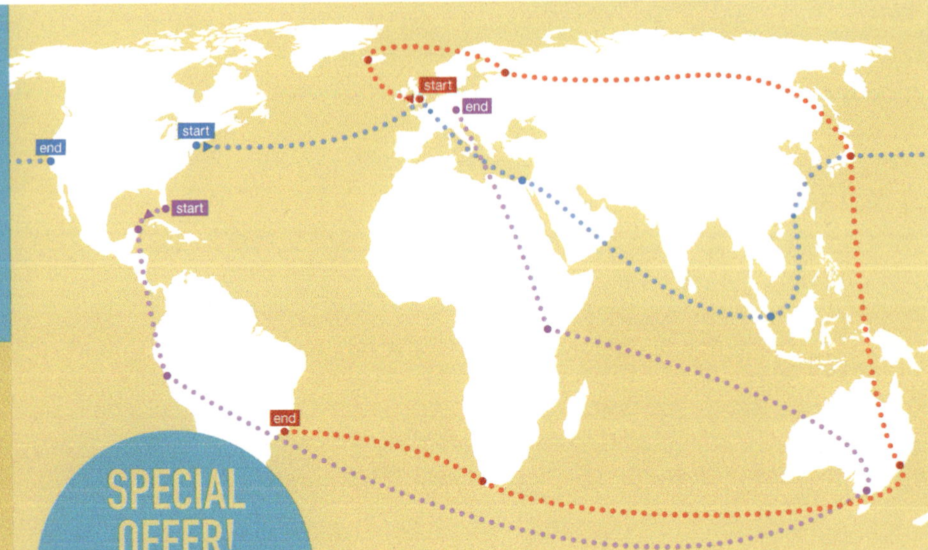

SPECIAL OFFER!

This week, choose our Nellie Bly Adventure and get 30 percent off your vacation.

THE NELLIE BLY ROUTE

In 1872, Jules Verne wrote about Phileas Fogg, an adventurer who traveled around the world in 80 days. But Fogg wasn't a real person, and nobody knew if this was actually possible.

In 1889, Nellie Bly, a 25-year-old American journalist, followed Phileas Fogg's route around the world. She went alone. She didn't take much luggage. She just took a large coat and a small suitcase. Her newspaper, the *New York World*, paid for her trip and told her story.

But a magazine, *Cosmopolitan*, sent their journalist, Elizabeth Bisland, to race against Nellie. Bisland left New York on the same day, but Nellie didn't know about it!

Car and plane travel didn't exist at the time, so Nellie traveled by bus, train and ship. She had many adventures, just like Phileas Fogg, and she sent her stories back home from every place.

Nellie crossed the Atlantic to London by ship. From there she traveled by train and ferry to northern France, where she met Jules Verne. She then continued by train to Brindisi, in Italy, where she took a ship to Egypt. She visited Port Said, in Egypt, where she rode on a donkey. Her ship then went to Singapore (where she bought a monkey), Hong Kong and Tokyo. Finally, the ship crossed the Pacific Ocean to San Francisco, where she took the train to New York. This took four days. She arrived in New York 72 days after her journey began. It was a new world record! Her story was in the newspapers.

And Elizabeth Bisland? She didn't join the celebrations. She missed her boat and returned to New York four days later.

Glossary

adventurer (n) someone who goes to exciting, unusual and sometimes dangerous places

route (n) a way that buses, trains, ships or planes travel regularly

C READ FOR DETAIL Read the article again. Number the pictures in the order they are written about.

a ☐

b ☐

c ☐

d ☐

e ☐

D READ FOR SPECIFIC INFORMATION Read the article again. Write down how Nellie traveled at each stage.

1 New York to London by *ship*
2 London to France by ____________
3 Tokyo to San Francisco by ____________
4 San Francisco to New York by ____________

E SPEAK Work in pairs. Answer the questions.

1 Do you know any of the places Nellie visited?
2 Do you know about any other famous journeys?

GRAMMAR

Simple past negative

A WORK IT OUT Complete the sentences with words from the text.

1 She ____________ much luggage.
2 Nellie ____________ about it.
3 Car and plane travel ____________ at the time.
4 She ____________ the celebrations.

B Read the sentences in Exercise A. Choose the correct options to complete the rule.

Simple past negative

To make the simple past negative we use *did / didn't* + *infinitive / base form*.

C Go to the **Grammar Hub** on **page VI**.

D SPEAK Work in pairs. Which forms of transportation did you use last year? Which didn't you use?

VOCABULARY

Travel phrases

A Complete the definitions with the words in the box.

arrive leave miss return take

1 ____________ (v) to be too late for a train, bus
2 ____________ (v) to use a particular type of transportation
3 ____________ (v) to go somewhere and come back
4 ____________ (v) to go away from a place
5 ____________ (v) to get to a place

B Go to the **Vocabulary Hub** on **page XVIII**.

PRONUNCIATION

Word stress: cities

7.4 **A** Listen and repeat the cities. Copy the word stress.

7.5 **B** Work in pairs. Add the cities in the box to the table. Then listen, check and repeat.

~~Ankara~~ Berlin ~~Cairo~~ Dubai London Miami Nairobi Paris Reykjavík Singapore Tokyo

Oo	oO	Ooo	oOo
Cairo		*Ankara*	

SPEAKING

SPEAK Work in pairs. Go to the **Communication Hub** on **page XXIV**.

Talk about a journey

7.3 A trip to remember

Talk about a vacation

G simple past questions **P** connected speech **V** verb phrases **S** guessing the meaning of unknown words

LISTENING

A Work in pairs. Look at the pictures. What country do you think it is? Why?

7.6 **B LISTEN FOR GIST** Listen to Emma talking to a colleague about a trip. What was unusual about it?

7.6 **C LISTEN FOR DETAIL** Listen to the conversation again. Check (✓) the things Emma did.

1 She decided to go to China. ☐
2 She went to Beijing. ☐
3 She saw pandas. ☐
4 She went sightseeing. ☐
5 She stayed with friends. ☐
6 She visited the Great Wall. ☐

7.7 **D** Listen to part of the conversation from Exercise B. Choose the correct meaning of the words. Use the information in the box to help you.

Guessing the meaning of unknown words

- When you don't know a word, listen for other words that you do know to help you understand.
- Think about: *What is the main idea? What is before and after the word that I don't understand?*

1 budget
  a the amount of money a person has
  b the amount of time a person has
2 destination
  a the place where someone is going
  b the place where someone is
3 surprise
  a something that we don't know about
  b something that we do know about

E SPEAK Work in pairs. Would you like to go on a mystery vacation? Why/Why not?

GRAMMAR

Simple past questions

A WORK IT OUT Look at the simple past questions from the conversation. Then choose the correct words to complete the rules.

Where did you go?
Did you visit the Great Wall?
Did you know the vacation was in China?

Simple past questions

1 To make *Yes/No* questions in the simple past we use ***do / did*** + subject + ***infinitive / base form***.
2 To make *Wh-* questions in the simple past we use question word + ***do / did*** + subject + ***infinitive / base form***.

B Go to the **Grammar Hub** on **page VI**.

C PRACTICE Reorder the words to write simple past questions.

1 to / Emma / China / did / fly / ?
Did Emma fly to China?
2 a lot of / visit / she / cities / did / ?
____
3 she / on / boat / a / sleep / did / ?
____
4 do / she / did / Beijing / what / in / ?
____
5 go on / mystery / vacation / a / did / she / why / ?
____

D SPEAK Work in pairs. Ask and answer the questions in Exercise C.

PRONUNCIATION
Connected speech

7.8 **A** Listen to the sentences. What do you notice about them?

1 Where did‿you go?
2 She went to‿a temple.
3 Did she stay‿in‿a hotel?

7.9 **B** Listen and repeat the sentences. Mark the links between the words.

1 Did Emma see a panda?
2 Did she stay with a family?
3 She visited a lot of cities.
4 Did she have a good time?

VOCABULARY
Verb phrases

A SPEAK Work in pairs. What do you think makes a great vacation?

B READ Read the three travel stories. Answer the questions.

1 What did TravelBob do every day in Ibiza?

____

2 What happened to Kate956 one evening in New York?

____

3 Where did LisaChorley lose her camera?

____

Kate956
January 7, 1:36

Last year, my husband and I went to New York. We **visited museums** and we **went shopping**. But New York is really big, and one night we **got lost**. After an hour, we were tired, so we stopped at a nice, small restaurant. We **ate some delicious food**, and then got a taxi back to our hotel!

LisaChorley
January 7, 1:41

Three years ago, I went to Thailand. I traveled around for two months, and I **met some really nice people**. In Bangkok, I went sightseeing and **took a lot of pictures**. But I **lost my camera**! I was really sad, but two days later a man brought it back. He saw a picture of me and my hotel!

C READ Read the comments again. Use the words in the box to create verb phrases.

eat get go have lose meet read swim take visit

1 ______________ in the ocean
2 ______________ shopping
3 ______________ museums
4 ______________ pictures
5 ______________ people
6 ______________ a book
7 ______________ lost
8 ______________ food
9 ______________ a good time
10 ______________ your camera

D SPEAK Work in pairs. Go to the Communication Hub on page XXIV.

SPEAKING HUB

A PREPARE Think of a vacation you went on where something unusual or funny happened. Write notes about the vacation using the ideas below.

- accommodations
- people
- place
- the ending
- the problem or a funny situation
- transportation

B DISCUSS Work in pairs. Ask and answer questions about your vacations using the prompts.

1 Where / go?
2 How / travel / there?
3 Where / stay?
4 What / happen?

Where did you go?

I went to Moscow.

C DISCUSS Work in groups. Tell your group about your partner's vacation. Take a group vote on the most unusual or funny vacation.

TravelBob
January 7, 1:25

One spring, I went to Ibiza with my family. The hotel was really nice, and we **swam in the ocean** every day. But on the last day of our vacation, we lost our passports and we couldn't fly home! We stayed for ten more days. We didn't have any money, but we **read a lot of books**! We **had a great time**.

Talk about a vacation

Café Hub 7.4 New York

Ⓕ– check in and out of a hotel Ⓟ– intonation in questions

COMPREHENSION

A ▶ 00:00–00:42 Work in pairs. Watch the first part of the video. Answer the questions.

1 Where did Sam and Zac meet?
2 What did Zac hate?
3 Why do you think he hated it?

B ▶ 00:42–04:38 Watch the second part of the video. Look at the hotel manager's checklist. Check (✓) the things Zac does. Put an ✗ on the things Zac doesn't do.

NEW HOTEL RECEPTIONIST

1. Greet guests correctly. ☐
2. Check guests' identity. ☐
3. Give correct information: breakfast time/price. ☐
4. Offer to help with bags. ☐
5. Check guests' room number and print out the bill. ☐

USEFUL PHRASES

A ▶ Complete the useful phrases with the words in the box. Then watch the video again and check your answers.

can it look mean new nice things what

1 Hey guys. How are ______________?
2 Hi! How's ______________ going?
3 I ______________, good afternoon, sir!
4 I'm so sorry, sir. He's ______________.
5 So, ______________ happened next?
6 OK, ______________ – it's fine!
7 You ______________ call me Sam.
8 Have a ______________ day!

B How do you say these useful phrases in your language?

FUNCTIONAL LANGUAGE

Checking in and out of a hotel

SPEAK Work in pairs. Practice the conversation. Change the words and phrases in **bold**. Use the words in the box to help you. Change numbers, times and prices, too.

dinner double evening
ID card ma'am would you like

Receptionist: Good **afternoon, sir**. How can I help you?
Guest: I have a reservation for a **single** room for **two** nights.
Receptionist: Could I have your **passport**, please?
Guest: No problem. Is **breakfast** included?
Receptionist: No, it isn't. Sorry. **Breakfast** is an extra **$14**.
Guest: What time is **breakfast**?
Receptionist: **Breakfast** is served from **7** till **11 am**.
Receptionist: **Do you need** help with your bags?
Guest: Great. Thanks.
Guest: Can I have my bill please?
Receptionist: Certainly, **Mr. King**. Which room was it?
Guest: Room **305**.

MILLY

SAM

NEENA

ZAC

GABY

PRONUNCIATION
Intonation in questions

7.10 **A** Listen and repeat the questions. Does the intonation go up or down at the end? Draw ↑ if the intonation goes up. Draw ↓ if the intonation goes down.

1 How can I help you? ___
2 What's your name, please? ___
3 Could I have your passport, please? ___
4 Is breakfast included? ___
5 What time is breakfast? ___
6 Do you need help with your bags? ___

7.10 **B** Listen again. Underline the words and syllables that are stressed in Exercise A.

C **SPEAK** Work in pairs. Practice asking the questions in Exercise A. Remember to use the correct stress and intonation.

SPEAKING

A **PREPARE** Work in pairs. Write a hotel check-in conversation. Use the information below. Use some of the phrases in Functional Language.

Guest

Ask about:

- Reservation for two adults and two children
- Wi-fi
- TV
- Cost of breakfast for you and children
- Restaurant opening times
- Check-out time

Receptionist

Give information about:

- Family room with one double and two single beds
- Free wi-fi 24/7
- All rooms have a TV
- Free breakfast for children
- Breakfast: $8.99 / 7 am to 11 am
- Dinner: $24.99 / 5 pm to 11 pm
- Check-out: noon

B **PRESENT** Practice your conversation. Perform it for the rest of the class.

Check in and out of a hotel

➤ Turn to page XXVI to learn how to write a short article about a travel experience.

Unit 7 Review

GRAMMAR

A Choose the correct words to complete the sentences.

1 Ten years ago, you ***take could*** / ***could take*** a ferry to the island from here.
2 You can't use the trolley in my town these days, but you ***can*** / ***could*** 50 years ago.
3 Before 2010, we ***couldn't*** / ***not could*** use the subway in my city.
4 When I had a scooter, I could ***got*** / ***get*** to school in 15 minutes.
5 ***I could*** / ***Could I*** ride a bicycle when I was six years old. How about you?
6 When we went to Venice, we ***couldn't saw*** / ***couldn't see*** any cars.
7 I couldn't ***swim*** / ***swam*** until I was ten years old.
8 When I was younger I ***could*** / ***couldn't*** run really fast, but I can't now!

B Complete the sentences with negative simple past form of the verbs in parentheses.

1 We ___*didn't travel*___ (*travel*) to Thailand.
2 They ____________ (*fly*) to Osaka.
3 He ____________ (*take*) the bus to Prague.
4 The people ____________ (*be*) friendly.
5 She ____________ (*stay*) in a hotel.
6 I ____________ (*have*) a good time.
7 I ____________(*have*) time to visit the Statue of Liberty.
8 She ____________ (*be*) on the same flight as me.

C Use the prompts to write simple past questions.

1 you / go on vacation / last year?
___*Did you go on vacation last year?*___
2 where / you / go?
____
3 how / you / get there?
____
4 where / you / stay?
____
5 you / go / with friends?
____
6 you / do?
____

D Think about your last vacation. Write short answers to the questions in Exercise C.

E SPEAK Work in pairs. Ask and answer questions about your last vacation.

A: Where did you go?
B: I went to Sweden. Where did you go?

VOCABULARY

A Label the pictures (1–4) with the words in the box.

bus ferry scooter trolley

1 ____________

2 ____________

3 ____________

4 ____________

B Choose the correct verbs to complete the text.

We [1]***left*** / ***missed*** New York City early in the morning and [2]***arrived*** / ***left*** in Bogotá five hours later. We [3]***took*** / ***left*** the train to the center. We stayed in Bogotá for two weeks. On the way home, we [4]***missed*** / ***arrived*** the train to the airport, so we [5]***left*** / ***took*** a taxi instead. We then [6]***took*** / ***returned*** a plane to Philadelphia.

C SPEAK Work in pairs. Tell your partner about the type of transportation you take every day. Then talk about the type of transportation you took on your last vacation.

D Complete the phrases with an appropriate verb.

1 _ _ _ lost
2 _ _ _ _ pictures
3 _ _ _ _ people
4 _ _ _ _ in the ocean
5 _ _ _ _ a good time
6 _ _ _ _ _ museums
7 _ _ _ _ your camera

FUNCTIONAL LANGUAGE

Complete the conversation with the words in the box.

346 bill (x2) minibar room stay taxi

Fumi: Hello. Can I have my [1]____________, please?
Receptionist: Good morning, sir. Which [2]____________ was it?
Fumi: Room [3]____________.
Receptionist: Did you have anything from the [4]____________?
Fumi: No, I didn't have anything.
Receptionist: Here you are. Here's your [5]____________. Did you enjoy your [6]____________?
Fumi: Yes, very much, thank you.
Receptionist: That's good. Do you need a [7]____________?

8 FOOD AND DRINK

One cannot think well, love well, sleep well, if one has not dined well.

Virginia Woolf

A selection of healthy fruits, vegetables and nuts.

OBJECTIVES

- talk about the food you eat
- talk about the food your family eats
- talk about ingredients and recipes
- order food in a restaurant
- write an online restaurant review

Work with a partner. Discuss the questions.

1. What's your favorite food?
2. Do you prefer eating at home or going to restaurants? Why?
3. Are you good at cooking?

8.1 I'm hungry!

Talk about the food you eat

V food and drink G countable and uncountable nouns; *some* and *any* P plurals

VOCABULARY
Food and drink

A SPEAK Work in pairs. Discuss the questions.

1 What's your favorite food?
2 What food do you have in your fridge at home?

B Go to the **Vocabulary Hub** on **page XIX**.

C SPEAK Work in groups. What kind of food is popular in your country?

GRAMMAR
Countable and uncountable nouns

A WORK IT OUT Read the conversation. Look at the nouns in bold. Which nouns are plural?

Waitress: Hi! What can I get you?
Customer: Hey. I'd like two **eggs**, a **tomato** and some **mushrooms**, please.
Waitress: OK. Anything to drink?
Customer: Uh … yes. Some **coffee**, please.

B Complete the rules.

Countable and uncountable nouns

1 We *can / can't* count countable nouns (e.g. eggs, tomatoes).
2 We *can / can't* count uncountable nouns (e.g. coffee, pasta).

C Complete the table with the words in the box.

apples bread butter a carrot chicken ~~coffee~~ ~~eggs~~ mushrooms an onion an orange hamburgers ~~a tomato~~

Countable singular	Countable plural	Uncountable
a tomato	*eggs*	*coffee*

D Go to the **Grammar Hub** on **page VIII**.

E SPEAK Work in pairs. Answer the questions.

1 How often do you drink tea or coffee?
2 How much fruit do you eat every day?
3 Are there any foods you didn't like when you were a child?

PRONUNCIATION
Plurals

8.1 **A** Listen and repeat. Do we always pronounce plural nouns the same way?

cakes, bananas, oranges

8.2 **B** Listen and complete the table with the words in the box.

apples ~~bananas~~ beans ~~cakes~~ carrots chips eggs mushrooms ~~oranges~~ potatoes hamburgers sandwiches

/s/	/z/	/ɪz/
cakes	*bananas*	*oranges*

LISTENING

8.3 **A LISTEN FOR GIST** Listen to Marta and Stefan. What is their conversation about?

8.3 **B LISTEN FOR DETAIL** Listen again and circle M (Marta), S (Stefan) or B (both).

Who …

1 can't eat pizza because they're on a diet? *M / S / B*
2 ate the chicken yesterday? *M / S / B*
3 doesn't want to eat vegetables for dinner? *M / S / B*
4 thinks they have a healthy diet? *M / S / B*
5 doesn't eat unhealthy food? *M / S / B*

C SPEAK Work in pairs. Answer the questions.

1 Do you want to try Stefan's diet? Why/Why not?
2 Do you think you have a healthy diet? Why/Why not?

A: I don't think I have a healthy diet. I eat a lot of fast food!
B: Really? I never eat fast food. I think I have a very healthy diet.

GRAMMAR

some and any

8.4 **A WORK IT OUT** Listen to part of the conversation between Marta and Stefan again. Then complete the sentences with *some* or *any*.

1 Is there ________ chicken?
2 There isn't ________ chicken. I ate it yesterday.
3 We have ________ mushrooms and ________ broccoli.
4 We don't have ________ apples or bananas.

B Look at the sentences in Exercise A. Complete the table with *some* and *any*.

some and *any*	
	countable and uncountable nouns
Positive +	1 ________
Negative -	2 ________
Questions ?	3 ________

Questions with *some*

When we make an offer or a request, we use *some* and not *any*.

*Do you want **some** bread?*

*Would you like **some** water?*

C SPEAK Work in pairs. Student A – go to the Communication Hub on page XXIII. Student B – go to the Communication Hub on page XXV.

SPEAKING

A PREPARE Think about the food you eat. Read the questions and write notes.

1 What do you normally eat for breakfast, lunch and dinner?
2 Which foods do you eat that are really unhealthy?
3 What did you eat for dinner last night?
4 Which do you prefer – cooking dinner or eating at restaurants? Why?

B SPEAK Work in pairs. Answer the questions in Exercise A. Try to ask for more information if possible.

A: I ate pepperoni pizza for dinner last night.
B: Really? Did you cook it at home or go to a restaurant?
A: I went to a restaurant with my friend.
B: Which restaurant did you go to?

Talk about the food you eat

Talk about the food your family eats

V containers P short and long vowel sounds G *much, many, a lot of*

Let's eat Around the world

How many people are there in your family? How much food do you eat in a typical week? Do you eat more packaged food or fresh food? What's your favorite food? And how much do you spend on food each week? Here, we take a look at food habits in different countries.

Ecuador

In Ecuador, most families don't eat any packaged food at all. People usually buy fresh food in local markets and they eat a lot of fruits and vegetables, as well as rice and potatoes. People usually buy food every day to cook at home. Lunch is an important meal and most children go home for lunch in the afternoon. Families usually eat together.

Average cost of food per week: $30
Popular food: rice, potatoes, chicken

The US

Most people in the US eat a lot of packaged food. They don't eat a lot of fresh fruit and they don't eat many vegetables. Meat is very popular here, as well as dairy products, like milk and cheese. Most Americans go to a big grocery store once a week to buy food. There aren't many markets, but some towns have a farmer's market once a week. A lot of families regularly eat at restaurants or eat fast food in front of the TV or in the car.

Average cost of food per week: $400
Popular food: corn, chicken, hamburgers

Italy

Italy is famous for its food, and for most Italians, food is a very important part of their day! Markets are very popular, but most people buy their food at a grocery store. Most people buy fresh bread every day, and they use milk mainly with coffee. Italians don't eat much packaged food, but people often buy cans of tomatoes and beans. The main meal of the day is usually lunch.

Average cost of food per week: $200
Popular food: pasta, rice, fish, bread

Source
https://www.dosomething.org/us/facts/11-facts-about-american-eating-habits

READING

A PREPARE Answer the questions. Use the places in the box to help you. Write notes.

in a market | in a grocery store | in local stores | online

1 Where do you buy fresh food? Why?
2 Where do you buy packaged food? Why?

B SPEAK Work in pairs. Look at the photos in *Let's eat - Around the world* and answer the questions.

1 What type of food can you see?
2 What kind of people can you see in the pictures?

C READ FOR GIST Read *Let's eat - Around the world* and check your answers to Exercise B.

D READ FOR DETAIL Read again and answer the questions.

1 Which meal is important in Ecuador?
2 Where do children in Ecuador have their lunch?
3 How often do most Italians buy bread?
4 In which country do people drink a lot of milk?
5 In which two countries do people eat packaged food?

E SPEAK Work in pairs. Answer the questions.

1 Why are the diets in Ecuador, Italy and the US so different?
2 Which diets are healthy? Why?
3 Which diet in the article is like yours? Which of the food in the pictures do you eat every week?

VOCABULARY
Containers

A Label containers (1–3) with the items in the box.

a bag of rice a bottle of fruit juice a can of tomatoes

B Go to the **Vocabulary Hub** on **page XIX**.

C SPEAK Work in pairs. What other types of food and drinks come in containers?

A: A carton of juice.
B: A can of soda.

PRONUNCIATION
Short and long vowel sounds

8.5 **A** Underline the vowels (*a, e, i, o, u*) in the words below. Then listen to the words. How is the vowel sound different?

1 fish 2 meat

8.6 **B** Listen and repeat the words. Are the vowel sounds long or short?

1 beef *long / short*
2 biscuit *long / short*
3 milk *long / short*
4 eat *long / short*
5 chips *long / short*

C Work in pairs. Discuss the questions.

1 How often do you eat chips?
2 Do you eat a lot of fish?

GRAMMAR
much, many, a lot of

A Look at *Let's eat - Around the world* again. Find and underline the phrases with *much, many* and *a lot of*.

B WORK IT OUT Look at the phrases you underlined in Exercise A. Complete the table with *much, many* and *a lot of*.

much, many and *a lot of*

	Countable nouns	Uncountable nouns
Positive +	She eats [1] *a lot of* bananas.	He eats [2] ______ pasta.
Negative -	She doesn't eat [3] ______ apples.	He doesn't drink [4] ______ coffee.
Questions ?	How [5] ______ cookies are there?	How [6] ______ rice is there?

C Go to the **Grammar Hub** on **page VIII**.

D PRACTICE Use the prompts to write questions with *How much* and *How many*.

1 bread / you / eat? *How much bread do you eat?*
2 tea / you / drink? ______
3 chips / you / eat? ______
4 meat / you / eat? ______
5 rice / you / eat? ______

E SPEAK Work in pairs. Answer the questions in Exercise D.

I don't eat much bread, but I eat a lot of pasta.

SPEAKING

A PREPARE Write questions to ask your partner about these things:

- his/her family (people, ages)
  How many people are there in your family?
- cost of food per week
  How much do you spend on food each week?
- food shopping (where? how often? what?)
- fresh food (fruits and vegetables, dairy, meat and fish)
- packaged food

B SPEAK Work in pairs. Ask your partner about the food they eat each week. Write notes.

C ORGANIZE Write a paragraph about your partner.

D PRESENT Tell the rest of the class about your partner. Do people eat similar or different food?

Talk about the food your family eats

8.3 Yes, chef!

Talk about ingredients and recipes

G *a*/*an*, *the*, no article **V** food preparation **P** consonant clusters **S** decoding

READING

A Work in pairs. Are the following sentences true for you?

1 I cook dinner every night.
2 I love making unusual dishes.
3 I buy a lot of food online.

B READ FOR GIST Read *Thanks for trying Homecook*. Which sentence best describes it?

1 It's a survey about people's cooking habits.
2 It's an advertisement about a food business.
3 It's a description of a cooking school.

C READ FOR DETAIL Read the advertisement again. Are these sentences true (T), false (F) or not given (NG)? Correct the false sentences.

1 *Homecook* delivers ready cooked meals to your home. T / F / NG
2 Customers can order a box for between two and four people. T / F / NG
3 Both Carlo and Frankie, who started the business, are Australian. T / F / NG
4 The business gets bigger every year. and now has over 100 staff. T / F / NG
5 Customers can order a maximum of 12 meals a week. T / F / NG
6 According to one customer, they now spend less on food with *Homecook*. T / F / NG

D Work in pairs. Look at the words in bold in the *Homecook* advertisement. What part of speech are they – nouns, adjectives or verbs?

E Complete the definitions with the words in Exercise D. Use the information in the box to help you.

> **Decoding**
>
> Noun, adjective, verb and adverb are all parts of speech. Thinking about parts of speech helps you work out the meaning of words.

1 ________________ sweet food after main meal
2 ________________ cooking instructions
3 ________________ one of the foods you use to make a particular meal
4 ________________ to take things like letters and goods to a place
5 ________________ extremely tasty or enjoyable

F SPEAK Work in pairs. Answer the questions.

1 Where do you buy fresh ingredients from?
2 Would you use *Homecook* to get fresh ingredients? Why/Why not?

Thanks for trying Homecook

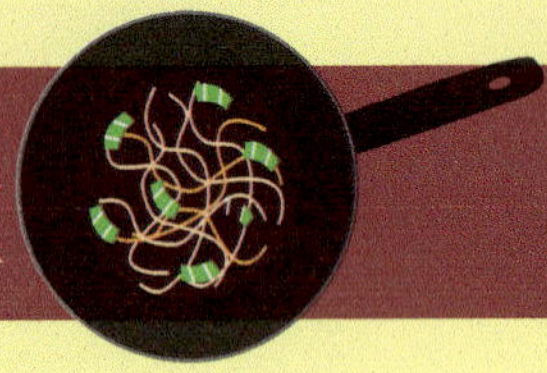

Our promise

With *Homecook*, you can cook quick, **delicious** meals at home with tasty ingredients.

Our offer

We offer boxes of fresh **ingredients** for a main course for two, three or four people. You can also order appetizers and **desserts**. Each box comes with a recipe. Follow the recipe to create a delicious meal.

Our story

Friends Carlo Vallone and Frankie Benn started *Homecook* in 2014 in Frankie's home city of Melbourne, Australia. Carlo, from Naples, is a chef and Frankie's speciality is business.

We started *Homecook* because we wanted to offer fresh ingredients that are ready to cook. And we did it. Last year we delivered over a million boxes!

How does *Homecook* work?

WE deliver thousands of boxes to homes around the country every week.
YOU choose from 12 delicious, healthy recipes each week.
WE deliver fresh ingredients and **recipe** cards for each meal you choose.
YOU cook, serve and eat!

"The ingredients are really good quality. We save money on our food shopping now. We're really excited when the box arrives each week."
Leanne, Geelong

GRAMMAR

a/*an*, *the*, no article

A WORK IT OUT Read the sentences from the *Homecook* advertisement. Match sentences (1–3) to rules (a–c).

1 Friends Carlo Vallone and Frankie Benn started *Homecook* in 2014 in Frankie's home city of Melbourne, Australia.
2 Each box comes with a recipe. Follow the recipe to create a delicious meal.
3 We deliver thousands of boxes to homes around the country every week.

> ***a*/*an*, *the*, no article**
>
> a ___ We use *a*/*an* the first time we talk about something. Then we use *the* to talk about it again.
>
> b ___ We usually use no article in front of names, places, companies and cities.
>
> c ___ We use *the* when there is only one or it is clear what is being talked about.

B Go to the Grammar Hub on page VIII.

VOCABULARY
Food preparation

8.7 **A** Listen to Carlo's recipe for hash browns and number the instructions 1–7.

Hash browns

Ingredients:
4 large potatoes
1 white onion
1 egg
salt and pepper
vegetable oil

Instructions:

__1__ **Grate** the potatoes and squeeze out the water.

____ **Peel** and **chop** an onion.

____ **Fry** for 2–3 minutes on each side, or until crispy.

____ **Put** one tablespoon of vegetable oil in a frying pan. When it's hot, put spoonfuls of the mixture into the pan. Make them flat.

____ **Crack** an egg into a bowl and **beat** it.

____ **Serve!**

____ **Add** the potato, onion, salt and pepper to the egg and **mix** them together.

B Match the instructions (1–7) in Exercise A with the pictures (a–g).

a ____

b ____

c ____

d ____

e ____

f ____

g ____

C **SPEAK** Work in pairs. What are your favorite dishes? Do you know how to cook them? Tell your partner.

A: I love pasta. I make it all the time.

B: Me too. I make a sauce with fresh tomatoes. You chop the tomatoes and fry them in olive oil with some garlic.

PRONUNCIATION
Consonant clusters

A Consonant clusters are groups of two or more consonant sounds. Underline the consonant clusters in these words.

1 bowl	3 fridge	5 shrimp
2 chips	4 mushroom	6 snack

8.8 **B** Listen and repeat the words in Exercise A.

SPEAKING HUB

A **PLAN** Work in pairs. Make a list of five meals that you can cook.

B **PREPARE** Choose one of the meals from Exercise A. List the ingredients and write a simple recipe for it.

C **PRESENT** Read your recipe to the class.

D **DISCUSS** Work in pairs. Which meals would you like to make? Which wouldn't you like to make? Why?

Talk about ingredients and recipes

Café Hub

8.4 More cheese

F– order food in a restaurant   P– stress and intonation

COMPREHENSION

A ▶ Watch the video. Complete the sentences with *Sam* or *Zac*.

1 ________ wanted to cook dinner.
2 ________ suggests they go out.
3 ________ orders chicken and rice.
4 ________ orders pasta and a large bottle of water.
5 ________ has a dessert.
6 ________ thinks ________ is strange.

B Test your memory! Check (✓) the ten items of food you can see in the video.

C ▶ **SPEAK** Work in pairs. Compare your answers to Exercise B. Then watch the video again and check your answers.

A: Was there any bread?
B: Yes, I think so. Were there any bananas?

FUNCTIONAL LANGUAGE

Ordering food in a restaurant

A Complete the conversations. Write *have*, *like* or the correct form of *be*.

Zac: Hi. A table for two please.
Waiter: Do you [1] ________ a reservation?
Sam: I [2] ________ afraid not. Could we [3] ________ a table over there, please?
Waiter: That [4] ________ fine, please come this way.

Waiter: [5] ________ you ready to order?
Sam: Yes, I think we [6] ________. I'll [7] ________ the chicken and rice, please. And a side salad.
Waiter: OK, one chicken, one side salad.
Zac: I'll [8] ________ the steak and fries, please.
Waiter: OK, one steak.
Zac: No wait. Sorry. I'll [9] ________ the pasta.
Waiter: Sure, one pasta. Would you [10] ________ something to drink?
Sam: Water, please.
Zac: Can we [11] ________ a large bottle of water?
Waiter: No problem.
Sam: Thanks.

Waiter: Would you [12] ________ to see the dessert menu?
Sam: I [13] ________ OK, thanks.

Sam: Can we [14] ________ the bill, please?
Waiter: Of course.

B ▶ Watch the video again and check your answers.

C **SPEAK** Work in pairs. Practice the conversation.

MILLY

SAM

NEENA

ZAC

GABY

PRONUNCIATION

Stress and intonation

A ▶ 01:38–02:10 Watch the scene in the restaurant again. Notice the word stress and intonation.

Waiter: Are you ready to order?
Sam: Yes, I think we are. I'd like the chicken and rice, please. And a side salad.
Waiter: OK, one chicken, one side salad.
Zac: I'll have the steak and fries, please.
Waiter: OK, one steak.
Zac: No wait. Sorry. I'll have the pasta.

B ▶ 01:38–02:10 Watch again and repeat the conversation. Copy the stress and intonation.

C SPEAK Work in pairs. Practice the conversation in Exercise A. Remember to use the correct stress and intonation.

MENU

MAIN COURSES

Chicken and rice
Steak with mushrooms and fries
Pasta with olives and tomatoes

SIDES

Fries
Rice
Salad

DESSERTS

Fruit salad
Cheesecake
Ice cream

SPEAKING

A PLAN Look at the menu. Underline the food you'd like to eat.

B SPEAK Work in pairs. Write and practice a conversation in a restaurant. Do these things:

- Order food from the menu.
- Change your order.
- Do or say something strange.

C PRESENT Perform your conversation for the class.

D Take a class vote for the best conversation and food selection.

Order food in a restaurant

➤ Turn to page XXVII to learn how to write an online restaurant review.

Unit 8 Review

VOCABULARY

A Match the food items in the picture (a–m) with the words in the box.

a banana ___ a loaf of bread ___ a slice of cake ___
carrots ___ cheese ___ chicken ___ an apple ___
a mug of coffee ___ eggs ___ milk ___
mushrooms ___ an orange ___ yogurt ___

B Choose the correct words to complete the phrases.

1 a *can* / *bottle* of beans
2 a *carton* / *bag* of fruit juice
3 a *bag* / *container* of yogurt
4 a *can* / *box* of tomatoes
5 a *bag* / *carton* of rice
6 a *jar* / *can* of mayonnaise
7 a *carton* / *bag* of chips
8 a *can* / *bottle* of lemonade.

C Complete the recipe with the verbs in the box.

add beat ~~chop~~ crack fry mix peel put

Spanish omelette

1 Peel and ___chop___ an onion.
2 ___________ the potatoes and cut them into small pieces.
3 ___________ one tablespoon of oil in a frying pan.
4 ___________ the onion and potatoes together for 20 minutes.
5 ___________ eight eggs into a bowl and ___________ them.
6 ___________ salt and pepper to the eggs and ___________ them together. Then add the mixture to the onions and potatoes.
7 Cook for 10 minutes, or until brown.

GRAMMAR

A Find and correct six mistakes in the conversation.

Eloise: What do you want to cook for the party?
Gemma: Hmm. How about fishes and beefs?
Eloise: Good idea! We can make some rices too.
Gemma: But Lola doesn't eat meats. She's vegetarian.
Eloise: We can make pastas with vegetable for Lola.

B Complete the sentences with *a/an*, *some* and *any*.

1 I have ___an___ apple and ___a___ sandwich for my lunch.
2 Do we have ________ mushrooms?
3 I want to make ________ pizza, but I don't have ________ cheese.
4 Is there ________ milk in the fridge?
5 Can you buy ________ potatoes at the store, please?

C Choose the correct words to complete the sentences.

1 Do you eat *a lot of* / *many* meat?
2 How *much* / *many* potatoes do you eat every week?
3 How *much* / *many* bread do we need?
4 We have *a lot of* / *many* eggs. Let's make a cake!
5 There isn't *much* / *many* fruit. Can you buy some?

D Find and correct the mistakes in four of these sentences.

1 Is there recipe for this meal?
2 My hometown is the New York City.
3 We need two lemons and orange.
4 They always put the ingredients at the top of the recipe.
5 My friend is very good at cooking delicious the meals.

FUNCTIONAL LANGUAGE

A Look at the conversation. Put the sentences in the correct order (1–7).

___ Waiter: Anything to drink?
___ Customer A: Yes, I'll have the chicken.
___ Customer A: Just water please.
___ Customer B: And I'll have the fish. No, wait. I'll have the steak.
_1_ Waiter: Are you ready to order now?
___ Customer A: Yes, we'd both like potatoes and vegetables please.
___ Waiter: Would you like anything with your chicken and steak?

B **SPEAK** Work in pairs. Student A is the waiter. Student B is the customer. Practice ordering food in a restaurant. Use the ideas in Exercise A to help you.

A: Are you ready to order now?
B: Yes, I'll have the fish, please.

9 SHOPPING

> If the shoe fits, buy it in every color.
>
> Anonymous

Shoppers on Black Friday in Maine, US.

OBJECTIVES

- talk about clothes and what people are doing
- talk about what people do at different times
- talk about shopping habits and tastes
- shop for clothes
- write a social media post

Work with a partner. Discuss the questions.

1. How often do you go shopping?
2. Look at the picture. Who do you think they're shopping for? Why?
3. Do you like shopping online? Why/Why not?

9.1 People watching

Talk about clothes and what people are doing

V clothes P /ɜːr/ G present progressive

VOCABULARY
Clothes

A Work in pairs. What clothes can you see in pictures (1–4)? Use the words in the box to help you.

cap coat jeans hat scarf shorts socks skirt sunglasses sneakers pants

1

2

3

4

B Go to the **Vocabulary Hub** on **page XX**.

C **SPEAK** Work in pairs. Look at the pictures in Exercise A.

1 Which clothes do you like? Why?
2 Which don't you like? Why?

PRONUNCIATION
/ɜːr/

9.1 **A** Listen and repeat. Notice that the underlined syllables are all pronounced as /ɜːr/.

early first learn prefer shirt

9.2 **B** Check (✓) the words that have the /ɜːr/ sound. Then listen, check and repeat.

☐ ear	☐ thirty
☐ her	☐ Thursday
☐ skirt	☐ we're
☐ there	☐ work

C **SPEAK** Work in pairs. Say this tongue twister.

I prefer to wear a shirt to work on Thursdays.

LISTENING

A What do you like to do when you are alone in a café? Which sentence describes you?

- I sit quietly and read.
- I usually use my phone.
- I watch the people around me.
- I call my friends.

9.3 **B** **LISTEN FOR KEY WORDS** Listen to Johan's conversation. Which of the activities in Exercise A does he do?

9.3 **C** **LISTEN FOR DETAIL** Listen again. Match the people (1–5) with their clothes (a–e).

1 customer	a pink dress
2 angry woman	b tie
3 tall man	c pajamas
4 short woman	d sneakers
5 young girl	e hat

D **SPEAK** Work in pairs. Answer the questions.

1 Do people in your town or city wear interesting clothes?
2 Do you know any celebrities who wear unusual clothes?
3 Why do you think people wear unusual clothes?

A: There is a charity run in my town every year. Lots of people wear funny clothes.
B: I think Lady Gaga wears unusual clothes.

GRAMMAR

Present progressive

A WORK IT OUT Look at the sentences from the conversation between Johan and Sophie. Underline the verbs.

1 What are you doing?
2 I'm having a coffee.
3 They're wearing really strange clothes.
4 No, the man isn't wearing pajamas.

B Choose the correct words to complete the rules.

Present progressive

1 We use the present progressive to describe ***what is happening now / routines***.
2 We make the present progressive with ***be + verb + base form / -ing***.
3 In present progressive questions, *be* comes ***before / after*** the subject.

Present progressive spelling

- We add *-ing* to most verbs in the present progressive.
  read – reading
  think – thinking
- With verbs ending in *-e*, we drop the *-e*, and add *-ing*.
  give – giving
- When the last three letters of a verb are consonant, vowel, consonant, we usually double the final consonant and add *-ing*.
  *run – ru**nn**ing*
  *stop – sto**pp**ing*
  Traveling is the exception to this rule in American English.

C Go to the **Grammar Hub** on **page X**.

D PRACTICE Use the prompts to write present progressive questions.

1 what / you / wear?
What are you wearing?
2 you / wear / warm clothes?
____
3 what book / you / read / at the moment?
____
4 you / eat / something?
____
5 what / you / think / right now?
____

E SPEAK Work in pairs. Take turns asking and answering the questions in Exercise D.

A: What are you wearing?
B: I'm wearing blue jeans, black sneakers and a white T-shirt. What are you wearing?

a

b

SPEAKING

A PREPARE Look at the pictures (a and b). Choose a person to describe. Think about:

- what they are wearing
- what they are doing
- where they are

B ORGANIZE Write notes about what you want to say.

This man is wearing sunglasses and a white shirt.
He's taking a selfie with his friend.

C SPEAK Work in pairs. Describe the person to your partner. Can they guess who you are talking about?

D DISCUSS Work in groups. Discuss the questions.

1 What do you think of the clothes people are wearing in the pictures above?
2 Would you wear the same clothes? Why/Why not?
3 What kind of clothes are fashionable in your country at the moment?

Talk about clothes and what people are doing

9.2 Job swap

Talk about what people do at different times

V present time expressions G simple present vs present progressive P /ŋ/

1

2

3

LISTENING

A SPEAK Work in pairs. Look at pictures (1–3). Would you like to do these jobs? Why/Why not?

9.4 **B LISTEN FOR GIST** Listen to the announcement. What is it about? Choose the correct answer.

a a competition
b a job offer
c a sale

9.4 **C LISTEN FOR KEY WORDS** Listen again and complete the sentences.

1 The prize money is $_________.
2 To win the money, shoppers must do a different _________ for one day.
3 The Clothing Department is on Level _________.
4 The Clothing Department is next to the _________.
5 Registration closes at _________ pm.

D SPEAK Work in pairs. Answer the questions.

1 What do you do? Are you a student? Do you have a job?
2 Do you like what you do? Why/Why not?
3 Do you want to change what you do?

READING

A Match jobs (1–6) with what the person does (a–f).

1 doctor	a teach children
2 mechanic	b plan events, book models
3 teacher	c fix engines
4 personal shopper	d help sick people
5 fashion show director	e take pictures
6 photographer	f give advice, choose clothes for shoppers

B READ FOR GIST Read the social media posts. Are Bryony, Lee and Adal enjoying their job swap?

C READ FOR SPECIFIC INFORMATION Read the posts again and answer the questions. Choose Bryony (B), Lee (L) or Adal (A).

1 Who loves his job swap? *B / L / A*
2 Who doesn't have a specialist to help her? *B / L / A*
3 Who wants to go back to his usual job? *B / L / A*
4 Who usually repairs things? *B / L / A*
5 Who usually helps sick people? *B / L / A*
6 Who is thinking about changing his job? *B / L / A*

D SPEAK Work in pairs. Answer the questions.

1 Do you think a job swap is a fun idea? Why/Why not?
2 Which job in *Job swap* would you like to try? Why?

VOCABULARY

Present time expressions

A Read *Job swap* again. Find and underline the present time expressions. The first two have been done for you.

B Choose the correct time expression to complete the sentences.

1 I spend a lot of time at the gym ***now / these days***. I'm trying to get in shape for the London Marathon next year.
2 I'm ***currently / today*** working at St. Crispin's Hospital in London. It's just for a few weeks.
3 I'm afraid Mr. Stevens isn't here ***at the moment / these days***. Can I take a message?

C SPEAK Work in pairs. Answer the questions.

1 What is your teacher wearing today?
2 What are you currently studying?
3 What are you doing more often these days?
4 What is your favorite TV show at the moment?

A: My favorite TV show at the moment is Game of Thrones. It's amazing!
B: Oh, really? That's my favorite show, too!

Job swap

GD **Greenfield Department Store**
October 23, 8:57 am

It's job swap day! We've asked the winners of our job swap competition (Bryony, Lee and Adal) to post updates here every hour to tell us how their new job is going.

Bryony Williams
October 23, 10:05 am

I'm enjoying my job swap, but it's completely different from what I usually do. I work as a doctor, but today I'm organizing a fashion show. It's hard work and there's a lot to do, but I'm having an interesting time. I love fashion and clothes, so I expected this to be easy, but it isn't. Today, I'm booking models and planning the event. The other job swappers have experts to help them, but I don't, so I'm feeling under pressure now!

Share Like Comment

Lee Cartwright
October 23, 10:17 am

Yesterday, I was a mechanic, but today I'm working as a personal shopper! I usually test cars and fix them, but today I'm giving people advice on buying clothes. I love my job at the garage, but I'm not enjoying this job at the moment. I can only write this now because my expert, Katrina, is talking on the phone. When she finishes, it's back to work for me. I don't want to do this anymore. I'm not having fun. I want to go back to my workshop.

Share Like Comment

Adal Khan
October 23, 10:21 am

I usually teach eight-year-old children, but right now I'm taking pictures of models. Currently, I'm working as a fashion photographer! I took over 200 pictures this morning and it isn't even lunchtime yet. I'm learning so many things and I'm having the best time. As a teacher, I usually tell people what to do at school, but today Santos, my expert, is teaching me. Who knows, maybe I'm starting a new career ... 😃

Share Like Comment

Glossary

career (n) a job that you want to do for a long period of your life
expert (n) someone with a particular skill or who knows a lot about a particular subject
swap (v) to give something to someone in exchange for something else

GRAMMAR
Simple present vs present progressive

A WORK IT OUT Read the examples in the box. Then choose the correct words to complete the rules.

Simple present and present progressive

1 We use the present progressive to talk about events that ***happen every day / are happening now***.
... but today I'm organizing a fashion show.
... so I'm feeling under pressure now.

2 We use the simple present to talk about ***events that happen every day / events happening now***.
I work as a doctor ...
I love fashion and clothes ...

Time expressions

Time expressions like *all day*, *every week* and *once a year* are used with the simple present.
I visit my grandmother once a week.
Adverbs of frequency (*always*, *usually*) are also used.
I usually test cars and fix them.
Time expressions like *today*, *now* and *at the moment* are used with the present progressive.
Today, I'm booking models.

B Go to the **Grammar Hub** on **page X**.

C SPEAK Work in groups. Discuss the questions.

1 What's something that you only do once a year?
2 How often do you speak to your parents?
3 What are you watching on TV at the moment?
4 What time do you usually finish work or college classes?
5 What's something that you never do?

PRONUNCIATION
/ŋ/

9.5 **A** Listen and repeat the pairs of words. Can you hear the difference between the final sounds?

1 ban / bang
2 thin / thing
3 win / wing

9.6 **B** Listen and repeat. All of the words have the /ŋ/ sound.

angry bank banking enjoying
finger having helping long shopping
taking talking thinking

SPEAKING

Work in pairs. Go the **Communication Hub** on **page XXV**.

Talk about what people do at different times

9.3 Shop till you drop

Talk about shopping habits and tastes

G object pronouns V stores and services P /ʧ/ and /ʃ/ S reading for genre

READING

A Work in pairs. Answer the questions. Use the words in the box to help you.

designer brands discount stores expensive things full price things good quality products local stores

1 What kind of things do you usually buy online?
2 What do you like spending money on? Why?
3 What don't you like spending money on? Why?

B Read *How to market your business* quickly. Where is it from? Who is the author writing to? Use the information in the box to help you.

Reading for genre

When you read something, it is important to know why the author wrote it. Think about:

- *Where is the text from (e.g. a website, magazine)?*
- *Who is the text for (e.g. students, doctors)?*

C READ FOR DETAIL Read the article again. Are the sentences true (T) or false (F)? Correct the false sentences.

1 Mike's store sells designer clothes. T / F
2 Mike isn't getting enough customers. T / F
3 Discount shoppers spend a lot of time in stores because they love shopping. T / F
4 Luxury shoppers don't worry about the price of things. T / F
5 Quality shoppers go to local stores because they are cheap. T / F

D SPEAK Work in pairs. Answer the questions.

1 What kind of shopper would be interested in Mike's business? Why?
2 What kind of shopper are you?

A: Mike could raise his prices. Then luxury shoppers might be interested in his business.
B: That's true. Quality shoppers might also be interested because they like to support local businesses.

How to market your business

Mike owns a small store. He spends all of his time working in it. It sells fruits and vegetables, cheese from a local farm, fresh homemade bread and delicious cakes. The store is on a busy road, full of cafés and restaurants. The local people have a lot of money and they know how to spend it. But Mike's business is slow. He's worried. He's trying different things to sell more food, but nothing is working. So what's he doing wrong? Maybe he isn't selling to the right people. It's the first rule of business: find out who your customers are, and listen to them. So, is business in your store slow? Read on to find out how to attract three kinds of shoppers.

Drop your prices

Discount shoppers like saving money! They like spending time in stores because they want to find everything at a good price. These shoppers like big grocery store markets and cheap local stores. Department stores are usually too expensive for them. They aren't interested in designer brands. They often shop online and travel to find the best price. They don't like paying full price for anything, and often buy clothes or big items when there's a sale.

Offer something special

Luxury shoppers love shopping, fashion and expensive products. Shopping is a serious hobby for them. They don't mind paying a lot for their favorite designer brands! Luxury shoppers hate cheap stores and prefer elegant department stores in the city center, where they can have a cup of coffee and meet their friends for lunch. Luxury shoppers buy what they want, when they want.

Offer quality

Quality shoppers look for products that they can use for many years and they are happy to pay a little more for something special. They look for good quality things in shopping malls. They also like local stores because they want to support businesses in their area. They often shop at markets, or at traditional local bakeries and butchers'. They also like to touch the things they are buying and they often spend a long time looking at them.

Which kind of shopper do you think would be interested in your business?

Glossary

brand (n) a product, or products, that has its own name and is made by a particular company
designer (adj) designer clothes are made by a famous designer and are usually expensive
local (adj) in or close to the area that you live in, or to the area that you are talking about
luxury (n) something expensive that you enjoy, but do not really need
quality (n) how good or bad something is
sale (n) an event or period of time when a store reduces some of its prices

GRAMMAR
Object pronouns

A Look at the sentences from *How to market your business*. Underline the prepositions and circle the object pronouns.

1. He spends all of his time working in it.
2. Department stores are usually too expensive for them.
3. Shopping is a serious hobby for them.
4. They like to touch the things they are buying and they often spend a long time looking at them.

B **WORK IT OUT** Choose the correct words to complete the rules.

Object pronouns

1. Object pronouns usually go at the ***beginning / end*** of sentences.
2. Prepositions usually go ***before / after*** object pronouns.

C Go to the **Grammar Hub** on **page X**.

D **SPEAK** Work in pairs. Answer the questions. Use object pronouns.

1. Do you have any brothers or sisters? How often do you see them?
2. What's your favorite movie? When did you last watch it?
3. Who do you like to go shopping with? Why?

I have one brother named Tom. I see him about once a month.

VOCABULARY
Stores and services

A Read *How to market your business* again. Find and underline eight words for stores or services.

B **SPEAK** Work in pairs. Where could you buy the things in the box? Use the words you found in Exercise A to help you.

apples a cake cheese a cup of coffee meat a pair of shoes a pizza a TV

C Go to the **Vocabulary Hub** on **page XX**.

D **SPEAK** Work in pairs. Answer the questions.

1. Do you prefer buying things online or in a store? Why?
2. Do you usually buy fruits and vegetables from a market or a grocery store? Why?
3. Is there a shopping mall near where you live? How often do you go there?

A: I prefer buying things online because it's quick and easy.
B: Really? I prefer buying things in stores because you can see things before you buy them.

PRONUNCIATION
/tʃ/ and /ʃ/

9.7 **A** Listen and repeat. Can you hear the difference between /tʃ/ and /ʃ/?

/tʃ/ choose, rich, chocolate
/ʃ/ shoes, shower, finish

9.8 **B** Complete the table with the words in the box. Then listen, check and repeat.

~~butcher's~~ ~~cash~~ change cheap choose fashion fresh lunch shoes touch

/tʃ/	/ʃ/
butcher's	*cash*

SPEAKING HUB

A **PREPARE** Work in groups. You are going to interview your classmates about their shopping habits. Think about:

- type of stores
- cost
- location

B **PLAN** Write questions for a shopping survey.

How often do you go shopping?
What kind of things do you usually buy online?
What do you like shopping for?

C **DISCUSS** Interview students in other groups. Write down their answers.

D **PRESENT** Get back into groups and compare your findings. Then present the information to the class.

Lots of people shop in grocery stores because it's easy and cheap.

Talk about shopping habits and tastes

Café Hub

9.4 Meeting Milly

COMPREHENSION

A SPEAK Work in pairs. Look at the picture of Milly's clothing store. Answer the questions.

1. How often do you go shopping for clothes?
2. Do you like clothing stores like Milly's?
3. What are your favorite kinds of clothing stores?

B Watch the video. Complete the sentences. Write *Milly*, *Neena* or *Zac*.

1. __Neena__ and __Zac__ are housemates.
2. ______ and ______ are old friends.
3. ______ and ______ meet for the first time.
4. ______ and ______ are American.
5. ______ and ______ are from Seattle.
6. ______ and ______ don't try on any clothes.
7. ______ and ______ leave the store together.

C SPEAK Work in pairs. Why can't Zac speak? How does he feel about Milly?

FUNCTIONAL LANGUAGE

Shopping for clothes

A Complete the conversations (A–F). Then watch the video again and check your answers.

A

Sales clerk: [1] ______ I help [2] ______?

Customer: No, I'm just looking, thank you.

B

Customer: Can [3] ______ try it [4] ______?

Sales clerk: Sure.

C

Customer: Where [5] ______ the changing [6] ______?

Sales clerk: They're over there next to the scarves and shirts.

D

Customer: [7] ______ do [8] ______ think, guys?

Sales clerk: It looks great!

E

Customer: Have [9] ______ got [10] ______ medium?

Sales Clerk: Yeah, I think so.

F

Customer: I [11] ______ take [12] ______ jacket, the skirt and the shirt, please. [13] ______ much [14] ______ that?

Sales clerk: That's £85, please. Thank you.

B Work in pairs. Practice the conversations in Exercise A.

MILLY

SAM

NEENA

ZAC

GABY

PRONUNCIATION
Connected speech

9.9 **A** Listen and repeat the questions. Is there a pause between the words connected with a ‿?

1 Can‿I try‿it‿on?
2 How much‿is‿it?

9.10 **B** Draw a ‿ to show the connected words. Then listen and check.

1 Can I try them on?
2 How much are they?
3 It's over there.
4 Your store is awesome!
5 Do you have an extra large?

9.10 **C** Listen again and repeat. Remember to use connected speech.

SPEAKING

A PREPARE Work in pairs. Look at the pictures. What do you like / not like about the clothes?

A: I really like the …
B: Do you? I think the …

B PLAN Work in pairs. Imagine you are in Milly's store. Student A – you are a sales clerk. Student B – you are a customer that needs help. Write a conversation.

Offer to help the customer.

Choose an item of clothing and ask to try it on.

Tell the customer where the changing room is.

Try it on and then ask for a different size.

Give the customer a different size.

Say you want to buy it and ask for a price.

Tell the customer the price and ask how they want to pay.

Buy the item and thank the sales clerk.

C PRESENT Perform your role play for the class.

Shop for clothes

➤ Turn to page XXVIII to learn how to write a social media post.

Unit 9 Review

VOCABULARY

A Choose the correct words to complete the descriptions.

He's wearing a [1]*suit* / *coat* and has brown [2]*shoes* / *boots*. His [3]*shirt* / *skirt* is white and his [4]*scarf* / *tie* is red.

She's wearing a blue [5]*dress* / *shirt*, with white [6]*sneakers* / *boots* and a pink [7]*sweater* / *coat*. She also has a yellow [8]*hat* / *bag*.

B Complete the sentences with the time expressions in the box.

at the moment	currently	today	this week	this year

1 Mom doesn't want to celebrate her birthday ______________.

2 I have a doctor's appointment ______________ at 3 pm.

3 I'm ______________ studying history at Cambridge.

4 I live with my parents ______________, but I want to move out soon.

5 I have so much work to do ______________! Five days isn't enough time.

C Complete the definitions with the words in the box.

bakery	bank	bookstore	butcher's
dentist's	hairdresser's	newsstand	pharmacy

1 ____________ a store that sells books

2 ____________ a store that sells meat

3 ____________ a place where you can borrow or save money

4 ____________ a place where you can have your teeth examined

5 ____________ a store that sells cakes, bread, pastry

6 ____________ a place where you get medicine

7 ____________ a place where you can get your hair cut

8 ____________ a place that sells magazines, newspapers, chocolate

D SPEAK Work in pairs. Answer the questions.

1 What kind of clothes do you wear at work/college?

2 What kind of clothes do you wear at home?

3 What are you wearing today?

GRAMMAR

A Choose the correct words to complete the sentences.

1 I usually *am working* / *work* on Saturdays, but I *'m taking* / *take* this Saturday off.

2 She *'s crying* / *cries* because romantic movies always *are making* / *make* her sad.

3 I usually *am going* / *go* camping, but this year I *'m staying* / *stay* in a hotel.

4 He *'s wearing* / *wears* white today, but he usually *is preferring* / *prefers* black.

5 I usually *am working* / *work* from home on Thursdays, but I *'m coming* / *come* in this week for a meeting.

6 She *'s meeting* / *meets* her friends tonight. I think they *'re going* / *go* to the movie theater.

B Complete the story with the correct form of the verbs.

My name is Marc Sands and I [1] ___work___ (*work*) in a clothing store. A lot of tourists [2] ______________ (*come*) to our store every day. At the moment, we [3] ______________ (*have*) a sale. It's only 9:30 am and people [4] ______________ (*come*) through the door already. The store [5] ______________ (*get*) busy.

C SPEAK Work in pairs and discuss things you do every day, and say what you are doing now.

D Complete the sentences with the correct object pronoun.

1 My brother knows a lot about luxury brands. He spends a lot of money on ___them___.

2 Alicia is an expert on saving money. I need to listen to ____________.

3 We need more staff. How can we get more people to work for ____________?

4 Tariq owns a busy café in the center of town. It is the most important thing to ____________.

5 My daughter has a new party dress. She wants to wear ____________ every day.

6 It's Mom's birthday on Saturday. Don't forget to call ____________!

FUNCTIONAL LANGUAGE

Match the beginnings of sentences (1–5) with the ends of sentences (a–e).

1 Can I	a are over there.
2 I'm looking for	b pants are over here.
3 Yes, our	c help you?
4 Can I try	d them on?
5 Yes, the changing rooms	e a pair of pants.

10 THE GREAT OUTDOORS

A young traveler at Iskanderkul Lake, Tajikistan

OBJECTIVES

- talk about and compare outdoor places
- talk about places around the world
- talk about living outdoors
- make and respond to invitations
- write a product review

Work with a partner. Discuss the questions.

1 Do you prefer cities or the countryside?
2 Look at the picture. Would you like to go there?
3 Which parts of your country are beautiful?

10.1 The right location

Talk about and compare outdoor places

V landscape features **G** comparatives **P** weak forms: /ə/ in *than*

FAMOUS MOVIE LOCATIONS

A lot of directors use studios or computers to make their movies. But some still like to use real places. Here are some famous movie locations that you can actually visit.

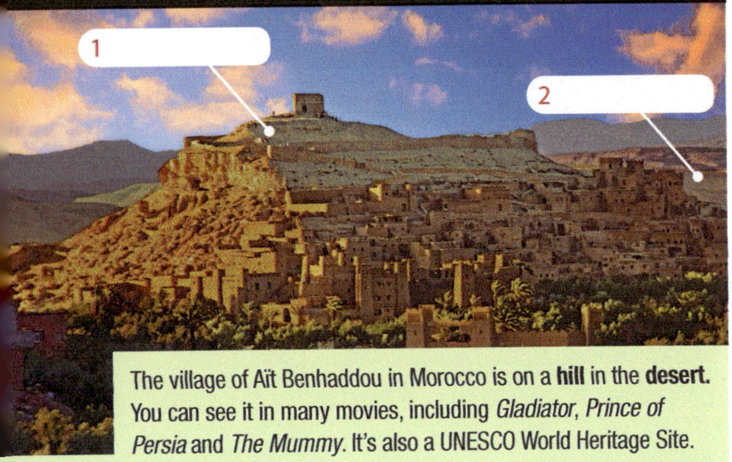

The village of Aït Benhaddou in Morocco is on a **hill** in the **desert**. You can see it in many movies, including *Gladiator*, *Prince of Persia* and *The Mummy*. It's also a UNESCO World Heritage Site.

The locations for the three *Lord of the Rings* movies are all in New Zealand. With its tall **mountains**, big **forests** and bright blue **lakes**, the Fiordland National Park was perfect for many scenes.

The **beach** of Maya Bay was the location of Danny Boyle's movie *The Beach*, with Leonardo DiCaprio. It's on the **island** of Koh Phi Phi Leh near Phuket. There are 32 islands here, surrounded by the beautiful blue **sea**.

Do you know this place? They made *Avatar* in this **jungle**, on the Hamakua Coast of Hawaii. This part of the island has around 200 cm of rain every year, and it's full of tall, green trees and beautiful **rivers**.

VOCABULARY
Landscape features

A Work in pairs. Look at the pictures in *Famous movie locations*. Where are they? What movies did they make there?

B Read the article quickly and check your answers to Exercise A.

C Read the article again. Label the pictures with the words in **bold**.

D **SPEAK** Work in pairs. Can you see any of these landscape features in your country? Tell your partner.

I'm from Spain. There are lots of beautiful beaches near Barcelona.

LISTENING
The movie location

10.1 **A** **LISTEN FOR GIST** Listen to Clarice talking about the locations for her movie. What is a location scout?

10.1 **B** **LISTEN FOR SPECIFIC INFORMATION** Listen again. Where did they film these scenes? Why? Write notes.

1 the beach scenes
2 the desert scenes
3 the jungle scenes

C **SPEAK** Work in pairs and discuss the questions.

1 What are some of the good things about filming in a studio?
2 What are some of the problems of filming in a real location (e.g. a city)?

A: I think it's easier to film in a studio.
B: I agree. You don't need to worry about the weather.

D **SPEAK** Work in pairs and discuss good movie locations in your country. Explain your ideas.

*Wadi Rum in Jordan is a great location for making movies. It's a desert. They made **Transformers: Revenge of the Fallen** there.*

GRAMMAR
Comparatives

A WORK IT OUT Look at these sentences from the TV interview with Clarice. Complete the table.

Mexico was **cheaper than** the US.

It was **more expensive** to film in the US **than** in Mexico.

Comparatives

	Adjective	Comparative	Rule
One-syllable adjectives	cheap	1 ______	We add 3 ______ + *than*
Adjectives with two or more syllables	expensive	2 ______	We add 4 ______ + adjective + *than*
Irregular adjectives	good	better	
	bad	worse	

B PRACTICE Complete the sentences with the comparative form of the adjectives in parentheses. Use the information in the box to help you.

Comparative spellings

For adjectives that end in *-e*, we add *-r*.

large → *larger*; *close* → *closer*

For adjectives that end with a consonant, we double the consonant and add *-er*.

hot → *hotter*; *big* → *bigger*

1 The mountains are ______________ (*cold*) than the desert.
2 Mexico is ______________ (*close*) to California than Morocco.
3 Hollywood is ______________ (*famous*) for movies than nature.
4 Mexico is four times ______________ (*big*) than Morocco.
5 Californian beaches are ______________ (*crowded*) than Mexican beaches.

C Go to the **Grammar Hub** on **page XII**.

D PRACTICE Use the prompts to write comparative sentences.

1 beautiful – New Zealand / Australia
New Zealand is more beautiful than Australia.
2 hot – Buenos Aires / Rio de Janeiro
____
3 long – the Amazon / the Nile
____
4 dangerous – the Sahara / Everest
____
5 cold – New York City / Moscow
____

E SPEAK Work in pairs. Look at the sentences in Exercise D. Say whether you agree or disagree.

A: New Zealand is more beautiful than Australia. What do you think?
B: I disagree. Australia has amazing beaches!

PRONUNCIATION
Weak forms: /ə/ in *than*

10.2 **A** Listen to five comparative sentences. Is *than* pronounced /ðæn/or /ðən/?

B SPEAK Work in pairs. Practice saying the sentences in Grammar Exercise B. Listen and check your partner's pronunciation. Be careful to pronounce *than* correctly.

SPEAKING

A PLAN Work in pairs. Choose two countries, two landscape features or two movies to compare. Then think of adjectives to describe them.

Canada: modern, cold, big ...
Thailand: beautiful, wet, traditional, interesting ...

B PREPARE Write sentences comparing the two things you chose in Exercise A.

Canada is colder than Thailand.

C SPEAK Work in another pair. Student A – tell your partner your ideas. Student B – say whether you agree or disagree. Take turns.

A: Canada is more modern than Thailand.
B: Hmm. I'm not sure. Bangkok is a very modern city.

Talk about and compare outdoor places

10.2 Where on Earth?

Talk about places around the world

V seasons and weather P /oʊ/ and /aʊ/ G superlatives

EXtreme places

This week, we look at some of the most difficult places to live on Earth. What's life like there? How do people survive in these places?

Yakutsk

It's winter in Yakutsk, Siberia. It's -42°C. It's snowing and it's foggy. Welcome to the coldest city on Earth. The lowest temperature in Yakutsk was -64°C. But about 270,000 people still live normal lives in this busy, modern city. They travel to work, go to school and meet friends. It's just like in any other city, except it's impossible to stay outside for too long. 'Yes, it's very cold, but I like it here,' says Nina. She's wearing a big fur hat, boots and a long coat, but she's smiling. 'Humans can survive anywhere,' she says.

Tristan da Cunha

A population of about 265 people live in the middle of the Atlantic Ocean. They are British, but they are 9,000 km from London. Their home is Tristan da Cunha. It's the world's most remote inhabited island. The weather is a little windy, but this isn't the problem. There isn't an airport, and the nearest mainland is South Africa, 2,430 km away. To get to the island, there's a boat from Cape Town. The journey takes six days.

So, how do people survive on this island? Well, there's electricity and the internet. There's a grocery store, too, but food is expensive, so most people on the island grow potatoes. Why do people stay when life isn't easy? Erik, a worker at the fish factory, says, 'It's so quiet and beautiful. We don't have the problems of the modern world here'.

*data true as of 2017

Kuwait City

It's a Saturday in Kuwait City – the hottest city in the world. About 2.4 million people live here, but you don't see anyone walking around. Why? Because it's 50°C and nobody wants to be outside.

The weather here is extreme. In the summer, it's hotter than the Sahara Desert. But this isn't the driest place on Earth – that's the Atacama Desert in Chile. In fact, there are a lot of thunderstorms in the fall.

What do people do here, then? During the hottest months, they live inside. Most people drive from their air-conditioned homes in their air-conditioned cars to air-conditioned offices and shopping malls. And there is another important thing. 'Water, water, water,' says Sharifa, an architect. 'We have to drink a lot!'

Glossary

extreme (adj) very great in degree
fur (n) the soft hair that covers the body of some animals
inhabited (adj) a place that is inhabited is a place that has people living in it
remote (adj) far away from other cities, towns or people
survive (v) to continue to exist, especially in a difficult or dangerous situation

READING

A Work in pairs. Look at the pictures in *Extreme places* and read the introduction. What problems do you think the people living in these places have? Write notes.

B READ FOR GIST Read *Extreme places*. Are there any ideas you didn't think of in Exercise A?

C READ FOR DETAIL Read again. Choose the correct answer a, b or c to complete the sentences.

1 Yakustsk is …
  a a quiet town.
  b a small village.
  c a busy city.

2 People in Yakutsk …
  a never go outside in winter.
  b go outside in the winter in warm clothes.
  c only go outside in the summer.

3 In Kuwait City, the streets are empty because …
  a it's too hot to go outside.
  b not many people live there.
  c people are at work.

4 There are a lot of cars in Kuwait City because …
  a it's a very big city.
  b it's very rainy.
  c people drive everywhere.

5 To get to the island, people on Tristan da Cunha have to …
  a fly from Cape Town.
  b take a boat.
  c fly from London.

6 People on Tristan da Cunha grow potatoes because …
  a food is expensive in the grocery store.
  b they can't grow other vegetables.
  c there isn't a store.

D SPEAK Work in pairs. Are there any extreme places in your country? Tell your partner about them.

VOCABULARY
Seasons and weather

A Look at the picture and answer the questions.

1 Which country do you think this is? Why?
2 Is the weather good or bad?
3 Is the weather like this in your country?

B Go to the **Vocabulary Hub** on **page XXI**.

C **SPEAK** Work in pairs. Answer the questions.

1 What's the weather like today?
2 What's the weather like in your country in each season?
3 What's your favorite season? Why?

PRONUNCIATION
/oʊ/ and /aʊ/

10.3 **A** Listen and repeat. Can you hear the difference between the sounds /oʊ/ and /aʊ/?

/oʊ/ snowing, go, throw
/aʊ/ cloudy, sound, brown

10.4 **B** Complete the table with the words in the box. Then listen and repeat.

~~around~~ cloudy ~~coat~~ grow home lowest now outside sound snowing town

/oʊ/	/aʊ/
coat	around

GRAMMAR
Superlatives

A **WORK IT OUT** Look at *Extreme places*. Complete the sentences with words from the text.

1 Welcome to ______________ city on Earth.
2 It's a Saturday in Kuwait City – ______________ city in the world.
3 But this isn't ______________ place on Earth – that's the Atacama Desert in Chile.
4 It's the world's ______________ inhabited island.
5 There isn't an airport, and ______________ mainland is South Africa, 2,430 km away.

B Complete the table. Use the examples in Exercise A to help you.

Superlatives			
	Adjective	**Superlative**	**Rule**
One-syllable adjectives	cold	1 ______ ______	We use *the* + adjective + 3 ______
Adjectives with two or more syllables	remote	2 ______ ______	We use *the* + 4 ______ + adjective
Irregular adjectives	good bad	the best the worst	

C Go to the **Grammar Hub** on **page XII**.

D **PRACTICE** Use the prompts to write superlative questions.

1 What's / high / mountain / in the world?
What's the highest mountain in the world?
2 What's / big / ocean / in the world?
____
3 What's / beautiful / place / in the world?
____
4 What's / good / movie / ever made?
____
5 Which / good / season to visit your country?
____
6 What's / bad / thing about your city?
____

E **SPEAK** Work in pairs. Ask and answer the questions in Exercise D.

SPEAKING

Student A – go to the **Communication Hub** on **page XXIII**.
Student B – go to the **Communication Hub** on **page XXV**.

Talk about places around the world

Talk about living outdoors

V phrasal verbs G verb + infinitive P weak forms: /tuː/ and /tə/ S identifying fact and opinion

READING

A Work in pairs. Tell your partner about the last time you got lost. What did you do?

A: I got lost on vacation in New York last year. I asked a policeman to help me!

B: Haha! I got lost in the mountains in France once. I called my friend for help.

B READING FOR GIST Read the article. Who is the article written for?

1 Someone who wants to go on vacation.
2 Someone who wants to go walking in a remote place.
3 Someone who wants to buy camping equipment.

C READ FOR DETAIL Read the article again. Match the beginnings of sentences (1–5) with the ends of sentences (a–e).

1 People die every year
2 The cold is more dangerous
3 You can't survive for a week
4 The safest way to drink water
5 Try to find

a is to boil it first.
b than almost anything else.
c because they don't prepare well.
d without water.
e plants to eat.

D Read these sentences from the article. Are they facts (F) or opinions (O)?

Identifying fact and opinion

Texts usually contain a mix of fact and opinion.

A fact is something that is true. Facts can include statements or statistics.

Most of them are between the ages of 20 and 29.

An opinion is what the speaker personally thinks about something.

Some people think it's important to take everything you need with you, like a tent, but I don't agree.

Opinions often include phrases such as: *I think …, I prefer …, I believe …, I feel …, In my opinion …, I agree, I don't agree / I disagree.*

1 I prefer to travel with only a few things and use what nature gives me. F / O
2 I believe that the best thing to do is to make a dry place where you can sleep. F / O
3 The night is much colder than the day. F / O
4 It's always safer to boil water before you drink it. F / O
5 I feel that the best thing you can do is learn to read the night sky before you leave. F / O

E SPEAK Work in pairs. Put Chuck's advice in order from the most important (1) to the least important (5). Explain your ideas.

I think finding somewhere to sleep is the most important advice because …

FIVE WAYS to survive in the wild

By top survival expert **Chuck Adams**

Every summer, hikers die because they don't prepare for their adventure. Most of them are between the ages of 20 and 29. So what happens if you get lost? Don't give up! I believe you can survive anywhere! Here are five tips before you set off on your next trip.

1 Build somewhere to sleep

Some people think it's important to take everything you need with you, like a tent, but I don't agree. I prefer to travel with only a few things and use what nature gives me. I believe that the best thing to do is to make a dry place where you can sleep. Put some pieces of wood against a tree and make a bed of grass on the ground. Also, one of the most dangerous things is the cold. The night is much colder than the day, so put on all of your clothes when you go to bed.

2 Make a fire

You only need two pieces of dry wood to start a fire! Check my Survival in the wild video on how to do this. Remember to add some big pieces of wood to keep you warmer for longer during the night.

3 Find water

Water is more important than food – you can only live for three days without water. It's better to drink water in rivers than water in lakes. It's always safer to boil water before you drink it.

4 Find food

We get most of our food from nature. Learn how to look for plants or flowers that you can eat. You can also catch and eat small animals. Watch my Survival in the wild video to learn how.

5 Read the sky

Use the North Star and the shape of the moon to help find out where you are. I feel that the best thing you can do is to learn to read the night sky before you leave.

Glossary

hiker (n) someone who walks long distances in the countryside for pleasure
nature (n) the physical world, including land, sea and all living things
survive (v) to continue to exist, especially in a difficult situation
the wild (n) an environment that is natural

VOCABULARY
Phrasal verbs

A Read the information in the box. Then read *Five ways to survive in the wild* and underline five phrasal verbs.

Phrasal verbs

Phrasal verbs have two parts, usually a verb and a preposition. The preposition often changes the meaning of the verb. For example, *give up* means 'stop doing something'.

A: *I'm tired. This race is hard.*

B: *Don't **give up**! We're almost there.*

B Complete the definitions with phrasal verbs from Exercise A.

1 ______________ to start wearing something
2 ______________ to stop doing something
3 ______________ to learn something
4 ______________ to leave
5 ______________ to try to find

C Go to the **Vocabulary Hub** on **page XXI**.

D Work in pairs. Write sentences using the phrasal verbs in Exercise B.

LISTENING

A Work in pairs. Look at *Marcus James: Survival Kit*. Do you think Chuck Adams uses any of these items? Why/Why not?

MARCUS JAMES: SURVIVAL KIT

10.5 **B LISTEN FOR GIST** Listen to an interview with survival expert Marcus James. Does he agree with Chuck Adams?

10.5 **C LISTEN FOR DETAIL** Listen again. Are the sentences true (T) or false (F)? Correct the false sentences.

1 The easiest way to make fire is from dry wood. T / F
2 Almost all hikers travel with energy bars. T / F
3 You can live for ten days without food. T / F
4 You should build a shelter to stay dry. T / F
5 You should take a lot of photos. T / F

D SPEAK Work in pairs. Put the items in Exercise A in order of most important (1) to least important (9). Then compare your list with another pair.

GRAMMAR
Verb + infinitive

10.5 **A** Listen to the interview again and complete the sentences.

1 Always **plan** __________ a few important things with you, like a pocketknife, a lantern and a phone.
2 For example, if you **want** __________ dry, take a raincoat.
3 You don't **need** __________ anything.
4 When you **decide** __________ hiking, tell someone where you're going.
5 And **remember** __________ warm.

B WORK IT OUT Look at the sentences in Exercise A and complete the rule.

Verb + infinitive

Lots of verbs in English are followed by ***infinitive / -ing***.
Examples include: *plan, want, need, decide, rememeber.*

C Go to the **Grammar Hub** on **page XII**.

PRONUNCIATION
Weak forms: /tuː/ and /tə/

10.6 **A** We pronounce *to* before an infinitive either /tuː/ or /tə/. Listen and repeat. Can you hear the difference?

/tuː/ to agree, to arrive, to open
/tə/ to believe, to prepare, to set off

10.6 **B** Listen again and complete the rules.

/tuː/ and /tə/

1 We say **/tuː/** before infinitives starting with a ***vowel / consonant*** sound.
2 We say **/tə/** before infinitives starting with a ***vowel / consonant*** sound.

SPEAKING HUB

Work in pairs. Go to the **Communication Hub** on **page XXV**.

Talk about living outdoors

10.4 Party invitation

F– make and respond to invitations P– stress and intonation

Glossary

cinema **(n) (British)** = movie theater **(n) (American)**

COMPREHENSION

A SPEAK Work in pairs. Look at the picture. What are Zac, Neena and Gaby planning? What do they have to decide?

B ▶ Watch the video. Choose the correct words to complete the sentences.

1 It's Sam's birthday *today* / *tomorrow*.
2 Neena has a birthday *present* / *card* for Sam.
3 Neena thinks the cinema is *boring* / *expensive*.
4 Gaby thinks a party is *cheaper* / *easier* than a restaurant.
5 Zac checks the *weather forecast* / *restaurant prices*.
6 They decide *to have* / *not to have* a picnic.
7 Zac suggests a surprise party *in the flat* / *at Sam's café*.
8 Neena tells Milly to arrive at *ten to* / *ten past* six.
9 Sam's parents *can* / *can't* come to the party.

C SPEAK Work in pairs. Answer the questions.

1 What is the final plan for the party?
2 Why does Zac shout when Sam arrives at the flat?
3 Why do Sam, Gaby and Neena laugh at the end?

FUNCTIONAL LANGUAGE

Making and responding to invitations

A ▶ Watch the video again. Check (✓) the invitations and replies you hear.

Inviting people	Are you free on Friday? We're having a party. ☐ Would you like to come to Sam's party tomorrow? ☐ We're holding a party for Sam tomorrow evening. Can you come? ☐
Saying *yes*	That sounds great. ☐ We'd love to come. ☐ Sure! I'd love to. ☐ That would be great. ☐
Saying *no*	Sorry, I'm busy. ☐ I can't come. I'm working. ☐ I'd love to, but I'm away. ☐

B SPEAK Work in pairs. Student A – invite your partner using the questions in Exercise A. Student B – reply using the phrases in Exercise A . Then swap roles.

MILLY

SAM

NEENA

ZAC

GABY

PRONUNCIATION

Stress and intonation

10.7 **A** Listen and repeat the replies. Copy the stress and intonation.

1 That sounds great.
2 We'd love to come.
3 Sure.
4 I'd love to.
5 Sorry, I'm busy.
6 I can't come. I'm working.

10.7 **B** Listen again. <u>Underline</u> the stressed word or syllable in the replies in Exercise A.

C SPEAK Work in pairs. Practice saying the replies in Exercise A. Remember to use the correct stress and intonation.

SPEAKING

A PREPARE Write notes about three activities to do with your partner.

- *See the new Avengers movie > Friday night.*
- *Go for a walk > Sunday afternoon.*
- *Play soccer > next Thursday.*

B SPEAK Take turns making invitations and saying *yes* or *no*. Use the phrases in the Functional language section and your notes to help you.

A: Would you like to see a movie with me this evening?
B: I'd love to, but I'm really tired.

C DISCUSS Work in pairs. Think about the last time you got an invitation. Did you go? If not, why not? Tell your partner about it.

A: I got an invitation to a work party last month.
B: Did you go?
A: No, I didn't. I was on vacation.

Make and respond to invitations

➤ Turn to **page XXIX** to learn how to write a product review.

Unit 10 Review

GRAMMAR

A Look at the advertisements for two apartments. Use the prompts to write comparative sentences.

$150 a night | Beautiful apartment, five minutes from the city center

Apartment / three bedrooms

★★★★ 3,256 reviews

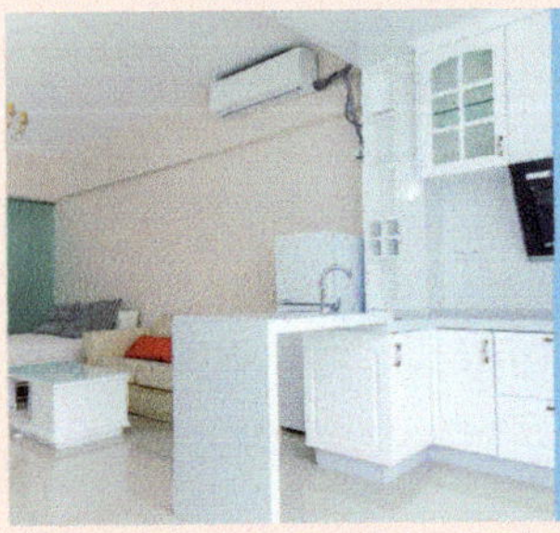

$60 a night | Excellent apartment, 20 minutes from the city center

Apartment / one bedroom

★★★★ 2,988 reviews

1 Apartment B / small / Apartment A
Apartment B is smaller than Apartment A.

2 Apartment A / expensive / Apartment B
____

3 Apartment A / good / Apartment B
____

4 Apartment A / big / Apartment B
____

5 Apartment A / close / to the city center / Apartment B
____

B Complete the sentences with the superlative form of the adjective in parentheses.

1 Death Valley is *the hottest* (*hot*) place in the US.
2 Lake Superior is ________ (*big*) lake in Canada.
3 Manchester is ________ (*rainy*) city in the UK.
4 Quito in Ecuador is ________ (*ancient*) city in South America.
5 Mount Kilimanjaro is ________ (*high*) mountain in Africa.
6 Tristan de Cunha is ________ (*remote*) island in the world.
7 Sushi is ________ (*good*) food in the world!
8 Laos is ________ (*beautiful*) country I visited in South East Asia.

C Choose the correct form of the verbs to complete the sentences.

1 I'm planning ***to go*** / ***going*** hiking this weekend.
2 I really enjoy ***to watch*** / ***watching*** horror movies.
3 Remember ***to take*** / ***taking*** a coat – it's cold outside!
4 It was raining, so I decided ***to take*** / ***taking*** the bus.
5 I keep ***to wake up*** / ***waking up*** at 6:30 am.
6 I really need ***to get*** / ***getting*** a haircut!

VOCABULARY

A Complete the descriptions with the words in the box.

beach desert forest hill island lake mountains river ocean

The [1] *desert* here is beautiful. The [2] ________ are very tall and there's snow on them. We can't swim in the [3] ________ because it's too cold.

We're camping here in the [4] ________. There are so many trees! We swam in the [5] ________ this morning; then climbed the [6] ________ next to the campsite.

This small [7] ________ is beautiful. We swam in the [8] ________ yesterday, then sat on the [9] ________.

B Look at the pictures. Complete the phrases.

1 It's *cloudy*.
2 It's ________.
3 It's ________.
4 It's ________.
5 It's ________.
6 It's ________.

C Complete the sentences with the phrasal verbs in the box.

found out give up look for put on set off

1 We ________ at five o'clock.
2 Don't ________! You're almost there.
3 Can you help me ________ my keys?
4 I just ________ that I failed my exam.
5 You should ________ a scarf. It's cold outside!

FUNCTIONAL LANGUAGE

Complete the conversation with the words in the box.

busy can't free sounds would

A: Are you [1] ________ tonight?
B: Why?
A: [2] ________ you like to go to the movies?
B: Sorry, I [3] ________. I'm [4] ________. Maybe another time.
A: How about tomorrow night?
B: That [5] ________ good. What's playing?

11 THE BODY

A woman doing yoga on an empty beach.

Health is the greatest possession.

Lao Tzu

OBJECTIVES

- talk about the body and health
- talk about your experiences
- talk about sports and hobbies
- ask for information
- write a recommendation on a forum

Work with a partner. Discuss the questions.

1. Read the quote. Do you agree?
2. Look at the picture. Is exercise part of your morning routine?
3. Where do you usually exercise?

11.1 Health tips

Talk about the body and health

V the body G *should* and *shouldn't* P sentence stress

VOCABULARY

The body

A Label the picture with the words in the box.

arm ear eye foot head heart neck stomach

The Body

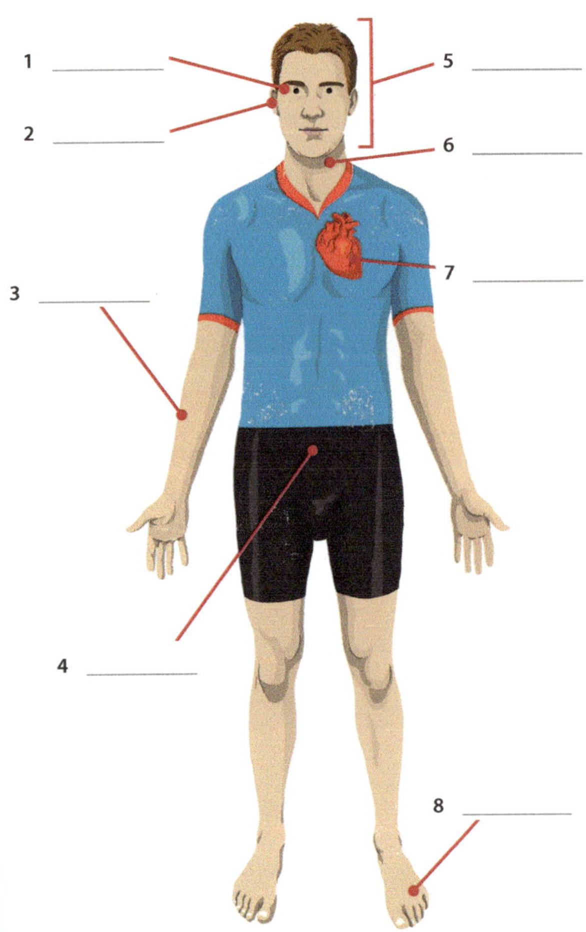

B Complete the sentences using the words for parts of the body in the box. There are two words you do not need.

blood brain hand legs nose skin

1 I run with my ______________.
2 I think with my ______________.
3 I smell with my ______________.
4 I hold a pen with my ______________.

Irregular plurals

We say *I have two feet* NOT *I have two foots*

C SPEAK Work in pairs. Take turns giving each other instructions.

A: Touch your neck.
B: OK … Point to your eyes.

LISTENING

A Work in pairs. Look at the items (1–7) from an article in a health magazine. Which parts of the body (a–g) do you think they match? Are these things good or bad for your body? Why?

1 a cell phone screen	a eyes
2 sleep	b brain
3 a firm bed	c blood
4 classical music	d back
5 a ball	e stomach
6 yogurt	f heart
7 coffee	g skin

11.1 **B LISTEN FOR KEY WORDS** Listen to Bianca and Ella talking about an article from a health magazine. Check your answers to Exercise A.

C LISTEN FOR DETAIL Listen again. Complete the sentences with no more than three words from the conversation.

11.1

your foot healthy coffee bed on your phone

1 Spending a lot of time ______________ is bad for your eyes.
2 Sleeping on a firm ______________ can help with a bad back.
3 Rolling a ball under ______________ helps blood flow around the body.
4 Eating yogurt can help keep your stomach ______________.
5 Putting ______________ on your skin can help make it softer.

D SPEAK Work in pairs. What things are good for you? What things are bad for you?

A: Cold showers are good for your skin.
B: Yes, and for your heart, too.

GRAMMAR

should and *shouldn't*

A WORK IT OUT Look at the sentences from the conversation between Bianca and Ella. Do we use *should* to give orders or to give advice?

You should listen to classical music every day.
You shouldn't drink too much coffee.

B Choose the correct words to complete the rule.

should and shouldn't

Should / Shouldn't is followed by ***infinitive / base form***.

C Go to the **Grammar Hub** on **page XIV**.

D SPEAK Work in pairs. Student A – ask for advice about your health. Student B – give your partner advice. Take turns.

A: I have breakout prone skin.
B: You should put coffee on it.

PRONUNCIATION

Sentence stress

A Listen and repeat the sentences. Is *should* or *shouldn't* stressed?

11.2

B Listen and repeat. Copy the sentence stress.

11.3

1 You should exercise every day.
2 You shouldn't eat much fat or sugar.
3 You should sleep eight hours every night.
4 You shouldn't use your phone at bedtime.
5 You should drink lots of water.

SPEAKING

A PREPARE Work in pairs. Look at the problems. What advice would you give each person?

1 My pants are too tight. *exercise more, eat less*
2 I can't see very well.
3 My head hurts.
4 I have a sore foot.

B PLAN Write two pieces of advice for each problem in Exercise A, one with *should* and one with *shouldn't*.

1 You should exercise more.
2 You shouldn't eat so much.

C DISCUSS Work in groups of four. Student A – read out a problem. Students B, C and D – give advice. Student A – choose the best advice for each problem.

Talk about the body and health

11.2 In it to win it

Talk about your experiences

G present perfect **V** irregular past participles **P** past participles

NoFear

Every week on *No Fear*, 20 players climb, swim and jump as they race to the finish line. Only three people make it to the final each week. In the end, there can be only one winner! Let's meet the three fastest people from last week …

Meet the players! >

Sam McGunn, 32

Sam is a firefighter. He works hard, but in his free time he's really active. He's jumped out of an airplane seven times, and he's run 23 marathons! Sam is very fit, but he's never won a competition. That's why he wants to win this. His wife, Tara, and son, Ben, are here to support him. What do you think? Is Sam the strongest player on the show?

Hana Hansen, 28

Hana hasn't played any sports in her life. But she owns a large farm and works on it seven days a week, 364 days a year. She often rides horses on the farm. Her husband, Raoul, spends a lot of time working in other countries, so she often has to take care of the animals, the house and their three young children on her own. Hana doesn't have any time for sports, but she's strong and she's a fighter. Can she beat Sam or Jude?

Jude Wexler, 31

Jude doesn't work, but he's traveled all over the world. He's climbed mountains in Africa and raced cars in the Middle East. Jude doesn't believe in hard work, he prefers to have fun. 'I travel all the time.' Have you ever flown an airplane? 'I have. I loved it.' Have you ever been to a gym? 'I haven't. I don't like exercising,' says Jude. 'To prepare for this type of challenge, you should do what you love. And I love having fun. I believe I can win.' Jude has won 14 competitions with this method. Can he make it 15?

Glossary

active (adj) someone who does a lot of different activities/sports and has a lot of energy and interests
challenge (n) something that needs a lot of skill and energy and determination to deal with or to achieve
firefighter (n) someone whose job is to put out fires and rescue people from dangerous situations

READING

A SPEAK Work in pairs. You're going to read an article about a TV show called *No Fear*. Look at the pictures. What do you think happens in the show?

B Read the article's introduction. Check your ideas from Exercise A.

C READ FOR GIST Read the text again. Complete the summaries with *Sam*, *Hana* or *Jude*.

1 ________ doesn't have a job and thinks the best way to win is by having fun.
2 ________ is fit, hardworking and has the support of his family.
3 ________ isn't into sports, but is strong and works all year to manage a large farm.

D READ FOR DETAIL Read again. Are the sentences true (T) or false (F)? Correct the false sentences.

1 Sam won seven competitions. T / F
2 Sam is married with a child. T / F
3 Hana is often home alone. T / F
4 Hana likes to ride around on her motorcycle. T / F
5 Jude likes going to the gym. T / F
6 Jude came in first in 14 competitions. T / F

E SPEAK Work in pairs. Which player do you want to win the competition? Why?

I hope Jude wins because I hate going to the gym, too.

GRAMMAR
Present perfect

A WORK IT OUT Look at the highlighted sentences from *No Fear*. Then choose the correct words to complete the rules.

Present perfect

1 We use the present perfect to talk about ***present / past*** experiences.
2 We ***say / don't say*** when in the past the action happened.
3 We make the present perfect with subject + *have* + ***simple past / past participle***.
4 We use ***ever / never*** in questions.
5 We use ***ever / never*** in negative sentences.

B Go to the **Grammar Hub** on **page XIV**.

C PRACTICE Use the prompts to write present perfect sentences. Use contractions.

1 I / not be / on a TV show
I haven't been on a TV show.
2 I / never / jump / out of a plane
______
3 She / climb / a mountain / three times
______
4 He / not try / any dangerous activities
______
5 They / visit / Africa / twice
______
6 I / never / watch / a game show
______

D SPEAK Work in groups. Write three present perfect sentences about yourself. Two true, and one lie. Read the sentences to the group. See if they can guess the lie.

VOCABULARY
Irregular past participles

A Complete the table with the correct forms of the verbs.

Irregular verbs		
base form	**simple past**	**past participle**
be	*was/were*	been
break	broke	broken
do	1 ______	done
eat	2 ______	eaten
3 ______	forgot	forgotten
go	4 ______	gone/been
have	5 ______	had
ride	6 ______	ridden
run	7 ______	run
8 ______	saw	seen
9 ______	took	taken
10 ______	won	won

11.4 **B** Listen and check. Then listen and repeat.

C Go to the **Vocabulary Hub** on **page XXII**.

D Go to **page IV** for a list of irregular verbs.

PRONUNCIATION
Past participles

11.5 **A** Listen and repeat the past participles. Notice how we say the underlined syllables.

/iːn/	/ən/	/ʌn/	/ɒn/
seen	broken	done	gone

11.6 **B** Add the verbs in the box to the table in Exercise A. Then listen, check and repeat.

eaten forgotten ridden run won taken

SPEAKING

A PLAN Write four questions with *Have you ever …?*

B SPEAK Interview people in your class and write notes. Use simple past questions to get more information.

A: Have you ever ridden an elephant?
B: Yes I have.
A: Really? Where did you ride one?
B: In Laos! It was amazing!

C DISCUSS Choose two people in the class to take part in *No Fear*. Say why you chose them.

We chose Agata because she has done more dangerous things than anyone else.

Talk about your experiences

11.3 Move it

Talk about sports and hobbies

G present perfect vs simple past **P** contractions **V** sports **S** understanding the sequence of past events

READING

A SPEAK Work in pairs. What do you think 'ultra-running' is?

B READ FOR GIST Read *Spotlight*. Choose the correct words to complete the sentences.

1 Ultra-running ***is / isn't*** running farther than a marathon.
2 Ultra-running is ***better / worse*** for you than running marathons.
3 You ***can / can't*** walk when you do an ultra-run.
4 Karina ***listens / doesn't listen*** to music when she's running.
5 You ***should / shouldn't*** eat a lot during an ultra-run.
6 You ***have to / don't have to*** start training when you're young.

C Read again. Number the events (1–5) in the order Karina did them. Use the information in the box.

Understanding the sequence of past events

To understand the sequence of past events in a text, think about:

- the order the information is stated
- time references (e.g. *2016, ten years ago*)
- sequencing words (e.g. *then, after that*)

a She did her first ultra-run. ☐
b Her children moved away. ☐
c She ran a marathon. ☐
d She ran in a competition in the desert. ☐
e She started running. ☐

D SPEAK Work in pairs. Would you try ultra-running? Why/Why not?

SPOTLIGHT

Karina Welch, ultra-runner

Are you bored of running marathons? Do you want to try something new? Ultra-running is becoming more and more popular. Ultra-runs are longer than marathons. They are usually in remote and beautiful places, like the Gobi Desert or the Rocky Mountains, so you can run and enjoy nature at the same time!

This week, we're talking to Karina Welch, an ultra-runner, who is 66.

So, Karina, when did you start running?
Twenty-five years ago, when I was in my late 40s. My children left home and I needed a way to spend my time, so I decided to start running. I began in my local park, then I ran a few marathons and finally I started ultra-running.

How many ultra-runs have you done?
I've done around 20 races. My first run was in 2009 and it was really difficult. Ultra-runs are different from marathons, but they're better for your body. You normally run in the countryside and not on hard roads.

Have you ever run a very difficult race? Where was it?
Yes, I have! Four years ago, I ran in the *Marathon des Sables* in the Sahara desert. I ran 250 km in six days, in very hot weather. I didn't actually run the whole time. I sometimes walked for a few kilometers, but that's normal in ultra-running. The important thing is to keep moving!

What do you do when you run for such a long time? Do you listen to music?
No, I like the silence, especially when I'm running in a very quiet place. I like listening to the birds and the wind. I usually eat a lot when I run. You need food to keep your energy levels up.

What are your tips for someone who is interested in ultra-running?
It's never too late to start! I didn't run when I was young and now I love it. Start with jogging, and slowly increase the number of kilometers. And always warm up before you run!

Finally, what do you like most about ultra-running?
I feel free. When I am running, I don't think about anything. It's just me, my legs and the sky.

Glossary

jogging (n) the activity or exercise of running at a slow steady speed
warm up (phr v) to prepare for a sport or activity by doing gentle exercises or practicing just before it starts

GRAMMAR

Present perfect vs simple past

A WORK IT OUT Look at the sentences from *Spotlight*. Choose the correct words to complete the rules.

I've done around 20 races.

My first run was in 2009.

Have you ever run a very difficult race? Where was it?

Present perfect and simple past

1. We use the present perfect to talk about an action in the past. We ***say / don't say*** when it happened.
2. We use the simple past to talk about an action in the past. We ***know / don't know*** when it happened.
3. We use time expressions, like *ago, in 2010, last week* with the ***present perfect / simple past***.
4. We often ask a general question about past experiences using the ***simple past / present perfect***.
5. We then use the ***simple past / present perfect*** to ask for more details or to give more details (such as *where, when, how*).

B Go to the **Grammar Hub** on **page XIV**.

C SPEAK Work in pairs. Take turns asking and answering questions. Discuss where and when you did them.

1. try / snowboarding?
2. run / in a race?
3. meet / a famous person?
4. win / a sports competition?

A: Have you ever tried snowboarding?
B: Yes, I have.
A: When did you go?
B: When I was in Andorra, last year.

PRONUNCIATION

Contractions

11.7 **A** Listen and read. Notice the pronunciation of the contractions.

1. a **I have** never been to Moscow.
   b **I've** never been to Moscow.
2. a **He has** never run a marathon.
   b **He's** never run a marathon.
3. a **We haven't won** the competition.
   b **We have not won** the competition.

11.8 **B** Listen and check (✓) the sentences you hear. Then listen again and repeat the sentences.

1. a ☐ I have been to New York five times.
   b ☐ I've been to New York five times.
2. a ☐ Elliott has never eaten sushi.
   b ☐ Elliott's never eaten sushi.
3. a ☐ She has not run a marathon.
   b ☐ She hasn't run a marathon.

VOCABULARY

Sports

A Complete the phrases with the verbs in the box.

do go play

B Go to the **Vocabulary Hub** on **page XXII**.

C SPEAK Work in pairs. Tell your partner what sports you play and how often you play them.

SPEAKING HUB

A PREPARE You are going to interview your classmates about sports and hobbies. Write five main questions.

Have you ever run a marathon?
When was the last time you went to the gym?

B DISCUSS Interview three students. Write notes about their answers. Try to ask follow-up questions to get more information.

A: What sports do you play?
B: I play soccer once a week and sometimes play basketball with my brother.
A: Do you play for a soccer team?
B: No, I just play with friends for fun.

C DISCUSS Have a class discussion. What is the most popular sport or hobby? Which is the most unusual? What is the most interesting thing that someone has done or made?

I think Pablo's hobby is the most unusual. He does Zumba … underwater!

Talk about sports and hobbies

Café Hub

11.4 Get fit

F– ask for information P– stress and intonation

COMPREHENSION

A ▶ Watch the video. Correct the six mistakes in the poster.

B ▶ **SPEAK** Work in pairs. Are the sentences true (T) or false (F)? Correct the false sentences. Then watch the video again and check your answers.

1 Milly's sitting in the park with her back against a tree. T / F
2 Neena is sitting in the kitchen. T / F
3 Neena did yoga before and fell over. T / F
4 The Yoga Yoga Yoga receptionist has short hair. T / F
5 At the beginning of the class, they put their hands on their chest. T / F

USEFUL PHRASES

A Change one word in each useful phrase. Use the words in the box.

calling coming eyes fired ~~last~~ legs

1 Oh, one final thing. *Oh, one last thing.*
2 Thanks for phoning Yoga Yoga Yoga. ______
3 What do you mean, you aren't working? ______
4 You're sacked! ______
5 Cross your arms. ______
6 Close your mouth. ______

B How do you say these useful phrases in your language?

FUNCTIONAL LANGUAGE

Asking for information

A ▶ 00.40–02:17 Complete Milly's questions. Then watch the video and check your answers.

1 What ______ is the next slow yoga class?
2 How ______ does it cost?
3 How ______ is it?
4 Are ______ any lockers for our bags?
5 How ______ people are in the class?
6 Can ______ book two places for Milly and Neena, please?

B Complete the questions. Use the questions in Exercise A to help you.

1 ______ do you open/close?
2 ______ reserve a badminton court?
3 ______ is it for one lesson?
4 ______ does it start/finish?
5 ______ teams are in the league?

C **SPEAK** Work in pairs. Student A – ask a question from Exercise A or B. Student B – make up an answer. Swap.

A: What time do you open?
B: 9 am every morning.

MILLY

SAM

NEENA

ZAC

GABY

PRONUNCIATION

Stress and intonation

11.9 **A** Listen and complete the questions.

1 What ______________ do you open?
2 How long does it ______________?
3 How much does it ______________?
4 ______________'s the instructor?
5 ______________ many people are in the class?
6 ______________ does it start?

11.9 **B** Listen again and repeat. Copy the stress and intonation.

C **SPEAK** Work in pairs. Practice asking the questions in Exercise A. Remember to use the correct stress and intonation.

SPEAKING

DISCUSS Work in pairs. Take turns booking a lesson using the information below.

Student A – call to book a lesson. Say who the lesson is for and ask about:

- time
- cost
- length of lesson
- name of instructor

Student B – look at the information in the advertisements and answer Student A's questions.

Urban dance class

All ages!
Teacher: Nino
Every evening 7–8 pm
Adult: $7.50 Students: $4.00
Only 12 places per class

Boxing class

Beginners!
Small classes – five people.
Teacher: Max
3 pm to 4 pm every day
$12.50

Swimming lessons

City swimming pool
Teachers: Ahmed and Fraser
Every Saturday
10:30 am to 12:30 pm
Adult: $5 Child: $2

Tennis lessons

One-hour lessons with your coach, Andy
Maximum of two people per lesson
Every afternoon from 2 to 4 pm
Adult: $16 Child: $9

Ask for information

➤ Turn to page XXX to learn how to write a recommendation on a forum.

Unit 11 Review

GRAMMAR

A Find and correct the mistake in each sentence.

1 You should to stop smoking.

______

2 You don't should eat junk food every day.

______

3 How often I should exercise?

______

4 Do you think I should to join a gym?

______

5 She shouldn't drinks so much coffee.

______

6 I shouldn't start going to bed earlier.

______

B Write the words in the correct order to make sentences.

1 jumped out of / three / He's / an airplane / times

He's jumped out of an airplane three times.

2 any / never / sports / He's / played

______

3 She's / won / never / a competition

______

4 you / been / Have / India / to / ?

______

5 you / Have / the new restaurant / to / been / in town / ?

______

6 been / Japan / times / I've / to / five

______

7 Have / an / you / elephant / ever / ridden ?

______

8 Mexican / never / eaten / food / She's

______

C Use the prompts to complete the conversation. Use the present perfect and simple past where necessary.

Eloise: you / ever / try / yoga? 1 *Have you ever tried yoga?*

Michael: Yes, 2 ______.

Eloise: when / you / try / it? 3 ______

Michael: Three months ago. I / go / to a class near my house. 4 ______

Eloise: you / enjoy / it? 5 ______

Michael: Yes, 6 ______. I want to go again. You / ever / try / it? 7 ______.

Eloise: No, 8 ______. Maybe we can go together.

D SPEAK Work in pairs. Talk about sports and exercise and then give some advice.

A: I want to exercise outside.

B: You should go running.

VOCABULARY

A Label the parts of the body (1–10) with words in the box.

arm brain eye foot hand heart leg neck nose stomach

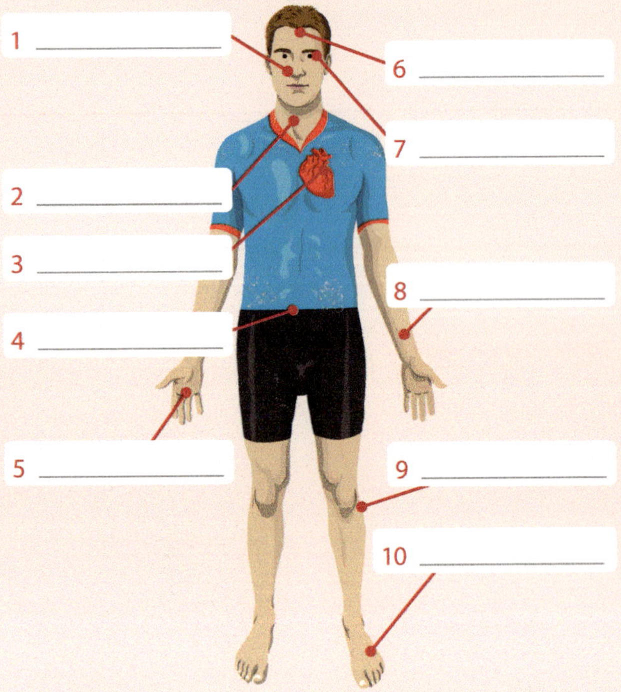

B Complete with the correct form of the verbs.

Ben is amazing. He's 1***did*** / ***done*** everything and he's 2***been*** / ***went*** everywhere. He's 3***flew*** / ***flown*** a plane and he's 4***seen*** / ***saw*** the Pyramids. I haven't ever 5***win*** / ***won*** a competition or even 6***ridden*** / ***rode*** a horse. But I have 7***broken*** / ***broke*** a bone, so I suppose that's something.

C Complete the table with the sports in the box.

bike riding ~~judo~~ badminton swimming ~~soccer~~ gymnastics basketball surfing tennis ~~running~~

play	go	do
soccer	*running*	*judo*

FUNCTIONAL LANGUAGE

Complete the questions (1–6) with the words in the box.

any how cost time ~~when~~ who

1 *When* 's the next exercise class?

2 What ______ does the gym open?

3 ______ long is the class?

4 How much does it ______?

5 Do I need to bring ______ equipment?

6 ______'s the class instructor?

12 MODERN LIVES

The best way to predict your future is to create it.
Abraham Lincoln

Jia Jia – a robot at a technology conference in Shanghai, China.

OBJECTIVES

- talk about future plans
- make predictions
- talk about social media habits
- show interest in something
- write a formal email

Work with a partner. Discuss the questions.

1 Where do you want to live in 10 years' time?
2 Look at the picture. Would you like a robot like this?
3 What do you want to do in the future?

12.1 Life's too busy

Talk about future plans

G *going to* P *going to*: weak and strong *to* V future time expressions

LISTENING

A Look at the picture. Work in groups and answer the questions.

- What problem does the person in the picture have?
- Are you a busy person? Why/Why not?
- How do you remember everything you have to do?

12.1 **B LISTEN FOR GIST** Listen to some friends talking. Who is the most organized person: Juliet, Mario or Kelly?

12.1 **C LISTEN FOR DETAIL** Listen again. Choose the correct answer to complete the sentences.

1 Juliet is working this weekend because
  a she always works on the weekend.
  b she was on vacation last week.
  c work is really busy at the moment.
2 Mario read an article about
  a how to work full time and study.
  b how to manage time.
  c how to get a better job.
3 According to the newspaper article, you should
  a make a short list of tasks.
  b make a long list of tasks.
  c never make a list of tasks.
4 Mario decides
  a to study this evening.
  b to learn to make lists.
  c to study in the mornings and work in the evenings.

D SPEAK Work in pairs. Do you agree with the advice? Why/Why not? What are some other ways to organize your time?

A: I agree with Kelly. You need to understand your body clock.
B: To organize my time, I use an app to make lists.

GRAMMAR

going to

A WORK IT OUT Read the sentences from the conversation. Underline the verbs. Does *going to* refer to the present or the future?

1 I'm going to try that idea at work next week.
2 I'm definitely not going to finish it.
3 Are you going to finish your essay this weekend?

B Complete the rules with *be* or *base form*.

going to for future intentions and plans
We use [1] ________ + *going to* + [2] ________ to talk about a future plan.

C Go to the **Grammar Hub** on **page XVI**.

D Complete the sentences with the correct form of *going to*. Use the verbs in parentheses.

1 I'm ________________ (go) to the movie theater on the weekend.
2 I'm ________________ (meet) friends after class.
3 I'm ________________ (relax) at home tonight.
4 I'm ________________ (have) chicken for dinner.
5 I'm ________________ (do) my homework this afternoon.
6 I'm ________________ (buy) a new car next year.
7 I'm ________________ (travel) around Europe this summer.

E SPEAK Work in pairs. Make the sentences in Exercise D true for you.

A: What are you going to do after class?
B: I'm going to meet my sister for lunch.
A: Oh, that sounds nice. I'm going to go to the gym.

PRONUNCIATION
going to: weak and strong *to*

12.2 **A** Listen and repeat the sentences. Notice that *to* sounds different in each sentence.

1 I'm going **to** finish my essay this weekend.
2 I'm not going **to** invite Paul and David to the barbecue.

12.3 **B** Read the sentences and circle /tə/ or /tuː/. Draw a ‿ to show any sounds that link together. Then listen and repeat.

1 I'm going to see the new Wes Anderson movie on the weekend. /tə/ /tuː/
2 Matt's going to study in Washington D.C. /tə/ /tuː/
3 I'm not going to eat anything until we get there. /tə/ /tuː/
4 He's going to open a restaurant in Cambridge. /tə/ /tuː/
5 I'm not going to stay long at the party. /tə/ /tuː/

C SPEAK Work in pairs. Practice saying the sentences in Exercise B. Listen and check your partner's pronunciation. Be careful to say *to* correctly and to link sounds with /w/.

VOCABULARY
Future time expressions

12.4 **A** Listen to Andrew talking to his manager, Yasmin. Check (✓) the things Andrew is going to do this weekend.

+ Add to list		
1	☐	Ask Jane about invitations
2	☐	Meet Chris
3	☐	Work at the conference

B Read the conversation between Andrew and Yasmin. Underline seven future time expressions.

Yasmin: So, Andrew. Are we all ready for the product launch next month?
Andrew: I think so. I still need to do a few things, like ask Jane about the invitations.
Yasmin: Are you going to speak to her soon?
Andrew: Yes. She's out at the moment, but I'm going to call her this afternoon.
Yasmin: Great. And what about Luis and Chris? Have you arranged a meeting with them?
Andrew: I'm going to meet Chris tomorrow, but I don't know about Luis. I think he's traveling at the moment. We've emailed each other a lot, but maybe I'll actually meet him one day!
Yasmin: OK. And what about the reception tonight? Are you going to be there?
Andrew: Yes, definitely. I'm looking forward to it.
Yasmin: I wanted to ask you … can you work this weekend? We need help with the conference.
Andrew: Uh, yes, that's fine.

C Use the prompts to write questions with *going to* and future time expressions.

1 What / do / tonight?
What are you going to do tonight?
2 How / travel / to class / next week?
3 What time / get up / tomorrow?
4 do / anything special / on the weekend?
5 go / on vacation / this year?

D SPEAK Work in pairs. Ask and answer the questions in Exercise C.

SPEAKING

A SPEAK Work in pairs. Student A – go to the **Communication Hub** on **page XXIII**. Student B – go to the **Communication Hub** on **page XXIV**.

B DISCUSS Write a list of five things you want to do soon. Share them with a partner. Ask and answer questions to find out more.

A: When are you going to start a photography course?
B: Next month. I love taking pictures!
A: Where are you going to do it?
B: At the art college.

Talk about future plans

12.2 Everything will be shiny

Make predictions

G *will* for predictions **V** collocations with *get* **P** contractions: *'ll*

READING

A Work in pairs. Look at the pictures (1–3). Describe the technology in each and how it might improve the world.

B **READ FOR GIST** Read *Future life*. Check (✓) the topics that Michael made predictions about.

- ☐ fashion
- ☐ virtual reality
- ☐ houses
- ☐ transportation
- ☐ video games
- ☐ robotics
- ☐ education
- ☐ soccer

C **READ FOR DETAIL** Read again. Are the sentences true (T) or false (F)? Correct the false sentences.

1. Michael gave the essay to his mother on her birthday. T / F
2. Michael thought people would walk more in the future. T / F
3. Michael thought that people wouldn't need jobs in the future. T / F
4. Michael's prediction about machines in stores came true. T / F
5. Michael thought that there would be robot teachers in 2018. T / F

D **SPEAK** Work in pairs. Answer the questions.

1. Which of Michael's predictions came true and which didn't?
2. Do you think that making predictions is useful?

A: Some of Michael's predictions came true. For example, every student here has a tablet.

B: Yes, but we don't all wear silver clothes!

FUTURELIFE About | Articles | Archives

What will the future be like?

No one knows, but we all like making predictions. In 1998, a young boy wrote an essay for a school competition with predictions about the year 2018. Michael Forster was ten years old when he wrote it. He didn't win the competition, but his mother saved the essay anyway and gave it to him on his 30th birthday. Some of Michael's predictions came true and others, well … read his essay below.

In 20 years' time, it will be 2018. I will be 30 years old. The world will be very different. Everyone will wear silver clothes and will have silver hair. All houses will be metal and everything will be shiny. Cars won't drive on roads; they will fly in the air. People won't walk because they will fly around with jetpacks instead. People won't get sick, hungry or thirsty. And they won't need to get money or have a job. Robots will do everything. They will take care of the people and get them everything they need. In stores, there will be robot sales clerks. Children will get to school on their jetpacks. At school, there won't be desks. Every student will have a computer. The teachers will be robots. The teacher-robots won't get angry with the students. Tottenham will win the European Cup.

Although Michael was wrong about a lot of his predictions – we don't all have silver hair, for example – some of his predictions were correct. Here at Futurelife, we love looking at past ideas about the future, so we asked Michael about his essay. 'I'm surprised that some of my ideas came true,' he said. 'We now pay machines for food at the grocery store. And many of us don't have desks; we work on computers all day.' What Michael's predictions show is that no one can predict the future, but a ten-year-old child's ideas aren't all crazy!

Glossary

essay (n) a piece of writing by a student about a subject
jetpack (n) a machine that someone wears on the back to make them fly
prediction (n) what you think will happen in the future

GRAMMAR
will for predictions

A Read these predictions about the future. Which ones came true? What has happened?

Computers are tools for scientists. Nobody will want to buy one for their home.
– **Henrik Andersson**, head of the American Telegraph Association (1943)

People want to go out to dinner, see their friends … maybe go to the movie theater. They won't stay at home watching TV.
– **Guy Chandler**, movie producer (1946)

Bitcoin is the future. In five years' time, Bitcoin will be the only way to buy things online.
– **Yoichi Katayama**, author of *The Eco Futurist* (2009)

Will we ever put a man on the moon? Maybe, but not for another 100 years.
– **Elliott Shaw**, writer for *The Boston Times* (1965)

Sadly, we won't have flying cars any time soon. They're just too expensive.
– **Sarah Kalensky**, writer for *The Forecaster* (2017)

B WORK IT OUT Choose the correct words to complete the rules.

will for predictions

1 For positive sentences, we use subject + *will* + ***infinitive*** / ***base form***.
2 For negative sentences, we use subject + ***won't not*** / ***won't*** + base form.
3 For questions, we use ***will*** / ***do*** + subject + base form.

C Go to the **Grammar Hub** on **page XVI**.

D PRACTICE Complete the sentences with *will* or *won't*.

In the future, …

1 there ______________ be cars. Everyone will have jetpacks.
2 students won't go to school. They ______________ study at home.
3 human teachers ______________ exist. All teachers will be robots.
4 other languages won't exist. Everyone ______________ speak English.
5 there ______________ be any books in schools. Every student will have a tablet.

E SPEAK Work in pairs. Do you agree or disagree with the predictions in Exercise D?

VOCABULARY
Collocations with *get*

A These sentences use phrases with *get*. Find two other sentences in *Future Life* that use phrases with *get*.

People won't ***get sick****,* ***hungry*** *or* ***thirsty****.*

And they won't need to ***get money*** *or have a job.*

Children will ***get to school*** *on their jetpacks.*

get

The verb *get* has three different meanings: **become** (*get sick*), **buy or obtain** (*get money*) or **arrive** (*get to school*).

B Go to the **Vocabulary Hub** on **page XXII**.

C SPEAK Work in pairs. Ask and answer the questions.

- What time you will get home today?
- What time do you usually get tired in the evening?
- What do you want to get the next time you go shopping?

I'll get home at 8 pm today. What about you?

PRONUNCIATION
Contractions: *'ll*

12.5 **A** Listen and repeat. Notice the difference between simple present and simple future with a contraction.

They like the movie. They'll like the movie.

12.6 **B** Listen and check (✓) the sentence you hear.

1 a ☐ We work together.
  b ☐ We'll work together.
2 a ☐ We leave early on the weekend.
  b ☐ We'll leave early on the weekend.
3 a ☐ We live in a big house.
  b ☐ We'll live in a big house.
4 a ☐ I travel a lot.
  b ☐ I'll travel a lot.

SPEAKING

A Work in groups. Think about the world in 2050. Make predictions about the things in the box.

houses technology the weather transportation

B PLAN In your groups, write predictions about what *will* and *won't* happen in 2050.

C DISCUSS Work with students from other groups. Discuss their predictions. Do you agree with them? Why/Why not?

D PRESENT In your new group, choose three predictions you think will come true. Present your ideas to the class and explain why you think they will happen.

Make predictions

12.3 Communication

Talk about social media habits

V internet communication P diphthongs G *might* S predicting

VOCABULARY

Internet communication

A SPEAK Work in pairs. Look at the infographic. How many of the social networks do you use? Do you use any others?

B DISCUSS Work in pairs and discuss the questions. Write notes.

Which network …

1 has the largest number of users?
2 is most popular with younger people?
3 is useful for professional people?
4 is useful to read the news?
5 is most popular in Asia?

C Quickly read the infographic and check your answers.

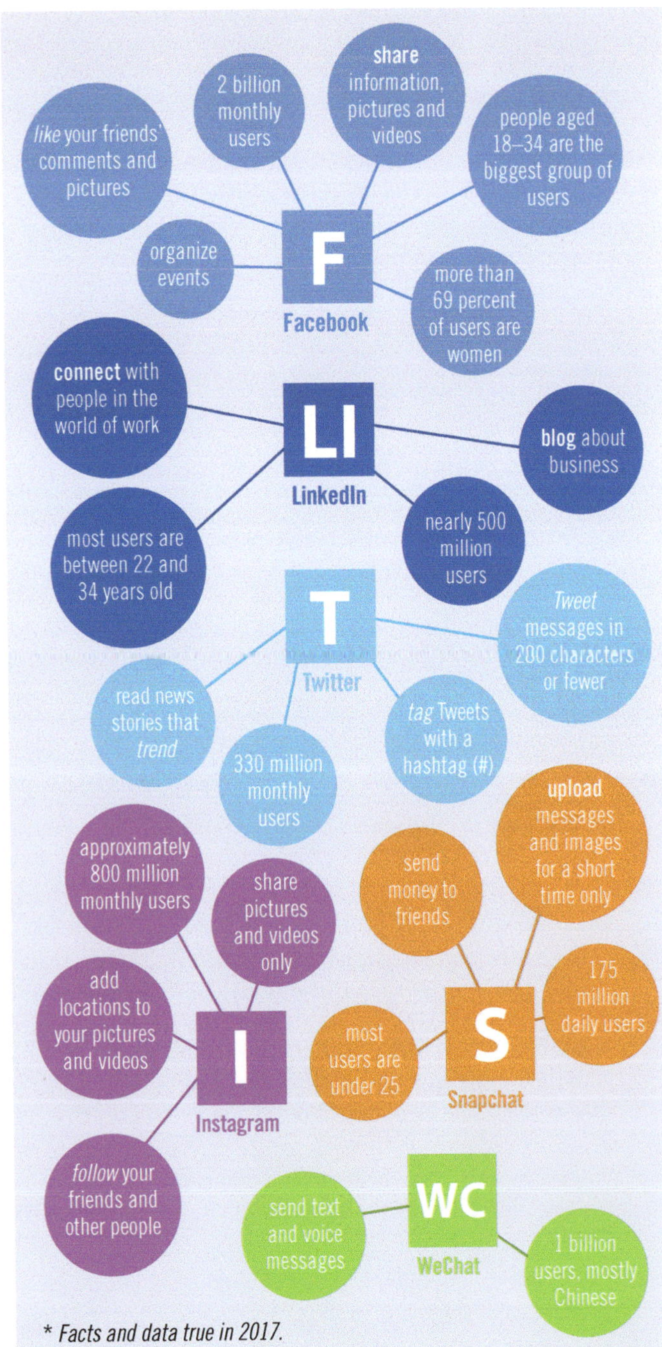

* *Facts and data true in 2017.*

D Match the words in the box to the icons (1–10).

blog chat connect follow like share tag trend tweet upload

1 ________ 6 ________
2 ________ 7 ________
3 ________ 8 ________
4 ________ 9 ________
5 ________ 10 ________

E Complete the sentences with words from Exercise D.

1 When I ________ a picture, I only ________ it with my friends.
2 I ________ comedians on *Twitter*. They ________ really funny comments and videos.
3 I ________ about music once a week.
4 On *Facebook*, I usually just '________' a few posts from family and friends.
5 I ________ with my friends on the phone not on social media.
6 I hate it when my friends ________ me in pictures.

F SPEAK Work in pairs. Which sentences in Exercise E are true for you?

PRONUNCIATION

Diphthongs

A 12.7 Listen and repeat the words in the table. Notice how we say the underlined letters.

/uw/	/eɪ/	/ɔɪ/	/oʊ/
new	place	boy	nose
/ju/	**/aɪ/**	**/aʊ/**	
cute	my	mouth	

Diphthongs are two vowel sounds that are said together. There are seven diphthongs in American English – **eɪ / aɪ / oʊ / ɔɪ / aʊ / ju /** and **/ uw /**. Practicing these sounds will improve your pronunciation.

B 12.8 Work in pairs. Add the words and phrases in the box to the table in Exercise A. Then listen and repeat.

true Facebook follow like mouse point users

LISTENING

A PREPARE You are going to listen to five people talking about social media. Look at the pictures and guess what their favorite social media network is.

Predicting

Before you listen, use information such as pictures, questions, what you already know to help you predict the topic or guess information.

12.9 **B LISTEN FOR GIST** Listen to the people. How many predictions in Exercise A did you get right?

12.9 **C LISTEN FOR DETAIL** Listen again. Choose a, b or c to complete the sentences.

1 Shani …
 a studied business. c teaches business.
 b runs a business.

2 Luke works in a …
 a café. b theater. c school.

3 Wai likes sharing his pictures on …
 a Facebook. b Instagram. c LinkedIn.

4 Jean has … grandchildren.
 a four b five c six

5 Maria likes that pictures only stay on Snapchat for …
 a ten years. b two hours. c ten seconds.

D SPEAK Work in pairs and discuss the questions.

1 Which age group do you think spends the most time on social media? Why?
2 How long do you think they spend on social media each week?

GRAMMAR

might

A WORK IT OUT Look at these sentences about social media. Then choose the correct words to complete the rules.

A: I might sign up to Snapchat so I can keep up to date!
B: A lot of the people at work also use LinkedIn, so I might set up an account, too.
A: I might try some other social media networks, but at the moment, I don't really know how to use them.

might

1 We use *might* for ***definite plans / possible plans*** or wishes.
2 We use *might* ***before / after*** the base form.

B Go to the **Grammar Hub** on **page XVI**.

C SPEAK Work in pairs. Think about your own use of social media. Tell your partner what you *are going to / might* use more (or less) in the future.

A: I'm so busy. I spend a lot of time on Facebook. I might try to use it less.
B: I'm going to start using Twitter.

SPEAKING HUB

A Go to the **Communication Hub** on **page XXIII**.

B Work in groups. Compare the results of your survey to the information in the infographic.

Like the infographic, we found that the most popular social network was Facebook. Some people in the class use Facebook and Twitter for their work, not LinkedIn.

Talk about social media habits

Café Hub

12.4 Party time

F– show interest in something P– stress and intonation

COMPREHENSION

A SPEAK Work in pairs. What is happening in each picture? Put the pictures in the order (1–6) you think they happen. Then watch the video and check your answers.

B SPEAK Work in pairs. Retell the story from the pictures.

FUNCTIONAL LANGUAGE

Showing interest in something

Complete the conversations with the words in the box. Then watch the video again and check.

did great love matter poor problem shame terrible thanks worry

Replying to bad news

Zac: Did you get tickets to the festival?
Sam: No, I didn't. All the tickets were sold out.
Zac: That's a [1] ______________. Sorry about that.
Sam: Ah, it doesn't [2] ______________.

Milly: I fell off my bike.
Gaby: Oh no! [3] ______________ you. Are you OK?
Milly: I'm fine. I fall off my bike all the time.
Gaby: Really? That's [4] ______________!

Replying to good news

Dad: Yeah, we're here for the weekend.
Sam: That's [5] ______________!

Apologizing

Milly: Hey! I'm really sorry I'm late.
Neena: No [6] ______________. You missed Sam's face. He was so surprised!
Milly: I'm so sorry I'm late.
Gaby: It's all right. Don't [7] ______________.

Giving compliments

Milly: That's a cool dress.
Gaby: Thanks, I [8] ______________ it.
Milly: Mmmm … and this cake is so good!
Gaby: [9] ______________. I made it!
Milly: [10] ______________ you? That's awesome!

MILLY

SAM

NEENA

ZAC

GABY

PRONUNCIATION

Stress and intonation

12.10 **A** Listen and repeat the replies. Copy the stress and intonation.

1	That's amazing!	5	That's a shame.
2	I love it!	6	It doesn't matter.
3	That's terrible.	7	No problem.
4	Poor you.	8	Don't worry.

B **SPEAK** Work in pairs. Student A – tell your partner some good or bad news. Student B – reply to your partner with one of the phrases in Exercise A. Remember to use the correct stress and intonation. Swap.

A: I got a new job.
B: That's amazing!

SPEAKING

A **PREPARE** Work in pairs. Write two conversations. Use the ideas below or your own ideas. Use the Functional language to help you.

Conversation 1

- You arrive late at the party because you got lost.
- You get lost all the time.
- You like your partner's jacket.
- You think the food is great.

Conversation 2

- You arrive late at the party because you left your bag on the bus.
- You lose things all the time.
- You like your partner's shoes.
- You think the music is great.

B **PRESENT** Practice your conversations. Then choose one and perform it for the rest of the class.

A: I'm really sorry I'm late.
B: It's all right – don't worry.
A: I got lost.
B: Oh no, poor you! Are you OK?

Show interest in something

➤ Turn to page XXXI to learn how to write a formal email.

Unit 12 Review

GRAMMAR

A Complete the conversation with the correct form of *going to* and the verbs in parentheses.

Erin: What [1] ___are you going to do___ (*you/do*) when you graduate?

Niall: I [2] ________________ (*work*) for my uncle's company in Australia for the summer, then in September I [3] ________________ (*start*) a course at the university there.

Erin: Wow! What [4] ________________ (*you/study*)?

Niall: Medicine. I [5] ________________ (*be*) a doctor one day! How about you? [6] ________________ (*you/look*) for a job?

Erin: No, I [7] ________________ (*travel*) around Asia with some friends for a few months.

Niall: Wow! That sounds amazing. You [8] ________________ (*have*) an amazing time.

Erin: Yes, and maybe I can visit you in Australia!

B Use the prompts to write predictions about the world in ten years' time. Then compare your ideas with a partner. Do you agree?

1 The weather / hotter
___The weather will be hotter.___
2 Food / more expensive
____
3 Clothes / cheaper
____
4 Robots / do a lot of jobs that humans do now
____
5 Children / use pens and pencils at school
____
6 People / drive electric cars
____

C SPEAK Work in pairs. Ask and answer questions about the future. Think about:

- your plans for the summer
- predictions for your life ten years from now

D Complete the sentences with *going to*, *might* or *will*.

1 I met Gianni on *Facebook*. We aren't sure yet, but we ___might___ meet face-to-face soon.
2 I start as my own boss next week, so *LinkedIn* ________ certainly be the social media network that I use the most.
3 I ________ send her a message now.
4 There's a new social media network. It ________ be popular in the future, but it will be difficult to catch up with *Facebook* and *Twitter*.
5 I think people ________ probably use social media more and more in the future.

VOCABULARY

A Complete the future time expressions with *a*, *e*, *i*, *o* or *u*.

1 I rarely exercise _o_n th_e_ w_e_ _e_k_e_nd.
2 I'm planning to buy a house n__xt y__ __r.
3 I'd like to climb Mount Everest __n__ d__y.
4 I have to go home s__ __n.
5 I'm going on vacation th__s s__mm__r.

B SPEAK Check (✓) the sentences in Exercise A that are true for you. Discuss your answers with a partner.

C Use the words in the box to complete the phrases with *get*.

home hungry lost money
organized sick ~~to college~~ wet

1 I usually get ___to college___ at nine in the morning.
2 It's raining. Let's go inside – I don't want to get ________.
3 I'm not very busy today. I think I'll get ________ early tonight.
4 Let's take a map so we don't get ________.
5 The five-list plan really helps me to get ________.
6 I always get ________ at about 3 pm.
7 Don't give her too many – she'll get ________.
8 I have to work. I don't get any ________ from my parents.

D Choose the correct words to complete the text.

I'm a designer and I have my own website. I [1]***connect*** **/** ***blog*** about art and design.

I sometimes use *Facebook* when I want to [2]***upload / chat*** pictures and [3]***follow / share*** them with my friends and family. It makes me happy when my friends [4]***blog / like*** my pictures. I have a *Twitter* account. I [5]***follow / upload*** my friends. They [6]***twitter / tweet*** a lot!

E Work in groups. Discuss the questions.

1 Who do you follow on social media? Why?
2 Do you think social media is the best way to connect with friends and family? Why/Why not?
3 What kind of things do you upload to social media?
4 Do you ever get angry when friends tag you in photos online?
5 What topic could you blog about?

FUNCTIONAL LANGUAGE

Match sentences (1–5) with replies (a–e).

1 I'm sorry I'm late.
2 I lost my phone yesterday.
3 I'm sorry, but I don't have any money.
4 My brother's going to be on TV tonight.
5 I passed all my exams.

a Don't worry. I can pay for this.
b Wow! That's great.
c That's OK.
d Really? That's interesting. Is he an actor?
e Oh, no. That's awful.

Endmatter Contents

Grammar Hub

7.1 *could*

	Positive	Negative
I/you/he/she/it/we/they	A hundred years ago, **you could see** a lot of trolleys in San Francisco.	**I couldn't get** to work because of the traffic jam.

	Question	Short answers	
I/you/he/she/it/we/they	**Could you run** fast when you were younger?	Yes, **I could**.	No, **I couldn't**.

- We use *could* to talk about general abilities in the past.
- In the negative, we can also say *could not*.

  *I **couldn't** drive. OR I **could not** drive.*

Be careful!

He could drive. NOT ~~He could to drive.~~ NOT ~~He could drove.~~

7.2 Simple past negative

	didn't + base form
I/you/he/she/it/we/they	**We didn't take** the trolley.

- We use the simple past negative to talk about things that did not happen in the past.
- We can also say *did not*.

  *We **didn't** take the trolley. OR We **did not** take the trolley.*

Be careful!

We didn't wait at the traffic lights. NOT ~~We didn't waited at the traffic lights.~~

7.3 Simple past questions

	Question	Short answers	
I/you/he/she/it/we/they	**Did they travel** to Beijing last year?	Yes, **they did**.	No, **they didn't**.

- We use simple past questions to ask about things that happened in the past.
- We can use question words with the simple past. These come before *did*.

  ***Where did** they go?*
  ***When did** she leave?*
- The verb *be* forms questions in a different way to other verbs.

  Was it expensive? NOT ~~Did it be expensive?~~

Be careful!

Did they go to New York? NOT ~~Did they went to New York?~~
Where did you go? NOT ~~Where you went?~~

7.1 *could*

A Use the prompts to write sentences with *could*.

Eighty years ago …

1 ✓ ride / a horse / into town

You could ride a horse into town.

2 ✗ take / a bullet train / across Japan

______

3 ✓ find / trolleys / in San Francisco

______

4 ✓ see / red double-deckers / in Mumbai

______

5 ✗ fly / quickly / across Europe

______

6 ✗ be / stuck / in a traffic jam

______

B Complete the paragraph using *could* or *couldn't*.

Two hundred years ago you [1] ______ travel around London on public transportation because … there wasn't any! In 1800, the city was still fairly small with only about one million people and most people [2] ______ walk from their home to their place of work. If you wanted to travel farther, you [3] ______ take a carriage pulled by horses, but only the very rich [4] ______ have their own private carriage. People [5] ______ cross the River Thames by taking a boat called a 'wherry'. Londoners [6] ______ take the subway until 1863 when the first station opened.

➤ Go back to page 63.

7.2 Simple past negative

A Complete the sentences with the simple past form of the verbs in parentheses. Use contractions.

1 It's OK. They *didn't miss* (not miss) their flight
2 I ______ (not arrive) home until midnight last night.
3 He ______ (not like) the food on the plane.
4 We ______ (not take) the train because it was very expensive.
5 Sarah ______ (not feel) well on the ship.
6 The children ______ (not enjoy) the journey. They were so bored!

B Complete the sentences with the negative form of the verbs in the box.

meet	pay	~~read~~	take	travel	write

1 We *didn't read* *Journey to the Center of the Earth* at school.
2 Jules Verne ______ about a real person.
3 Nellie Bly ______ to India.
4 She ______ a lot of luggage with her.
5 She ______ for the trip. The *New York World* paid.
6 Nellie ______ Elizabeth Bisland on her journey.

➤ Go back to page 65.

7.3 Simple past questions

A Use the prompts to write questions and short answers.

1 they / go / with their friends
Did they go with their friends? (?)
Yes, they did. (+)

2 you / visit / a lot of cities
______ (?)
______ (-)

3 she / meet / many people
______ (?)
______ (+)

4 your company / pay / for the flight
______ (?)
______ (+)

5 they / visit / the Eiffel Tower
______ (?)
______ (-)

6 you / sleep / on the plane
______ (?)
______ (-)

B Complete the questions with *you* and a verb from the box.

eat	get	go	~~have~~	stay	swim	travel	visit

1 *Did you have* a good vacation?
2 Where ______ on vacation this year?
3 How ______ there? By plane?
4 ______ any interesting museums?
5 ______ any local food?
6 ______ in the ocean?
7 How long ______ for?
8 ______ by bus or train?

➤ Go back to page 66.

Grammar Hub

8.1 Countable and uncountable nouns; *some* and *any*

Singular countable nouns	Plural countable nouns	Uncountable nouns
an apple	apples	bread
a banana	bananas	butter
a carrot	carrots	cheese
an egg	eggs	chicken
a mushroom	mushrooms	fish
an orange	oranges	lettuce
a potato	potatoes	milk
a tomato	tomatoes	rice
		water

- Countable nouns are nouns you can count.
- Most nouns are countable. They can be singular or plural.

  a banana *six bananas*
- Uncountable nouns don't have a plural form and we can't count uncountable nouns.

  beef NOT ~~*beefs*~~ OR ~~*one beef, two beefs*~~

	Singular countable nouns	Plural countable nouns	Uncountable nouns
Positive	*a/an*	*some*	*some*
	I have **a banana** in my bag. I had **an apple** for breakfast.	There are **some apples** in the fridge. I have **some tomatoes** for the salad.	I can buy **some milk** on the way home.
Negative	*a/an*	*any*	*any*
	I don't have **a banana**. No, I don't want **an orange**, thank you.	There aren't **any burgers** left. I'm afraid we don't have **any mushrooms**.	Sorry, I don't have **any tea**.
Question	*a/an*	*any*	*any*
	Do you want **a banana**? Is there **an onion** in this recipe?	Do we have **any mushrooms**? Are there **any sausages** left?	Do you have **any cake**? Is there **any yogurt** in the fridge?

Be careful!

- With questions, we often use *some* when we make an offer.

  Do you want some bread?
- We use *some* not *any* when we make a request.

  Can I have some rice, please? NOT ~~*Can I have any rice, please?*~~

8.2 *much, many, a lot of*

	Countable nouns	Uncountable nouns
Positive	*a lot of*	*a lot of*
	There are **a lot of carrots** in this recipe!	She drinks **a lot of coffee**.
Negative	*not many*	*not much*
	We don't have **many tomatoes**.	There isn't **much milk** left.
Question	*How many?*	*How much?*
	How many potatoes do we need?	**How much pasta** do you want?

- We use *a lot of* with countable and uncountable nouns.
- We use *many* with countable nouns.
- We use *much* with uncountable nouns.

Be careful!

- We use **a lot of** for a large amount.

  There are a lot of eggs in this recipe.
- We use **some** for a medium amount.

  There is some milk in this recipe.
- We use **not many/much** for a small amount.

  There isn't much sugar in this recipe.

8.3 *a/an, the*, no article

a/an	We use *a/an* the first time we talk about a singular noun.	I have **a recipe** for lasagna. There's **an onion** in the cupboard over there.
the	We use *the* with singular nouns when it is clear what we are talking about or when there is only one.	Fry **the onion** for five minutes. Where's **the waitress**?
	We use *the* with plural nouns when it is clear what we are talking about.	**The ingredients** for this recipe are unusual.
no article	We use no article with the names of people, companies, cities and countries (except *the UK, the US, the Netherlands*).	This is **Erica**. She's a chef from **Sydney, Australia**.
	We use no article when we talk about things in general.	Do you like **pizza**? **Chips** are not very healthy.

8.1 Countable and uncountable nouns; *some* and *any*

A Choose the correct options to complete the sentences.

1. I'm a vegetarian so I don't eat *meat / meats*.
2. Would you like some *chip / chips*?
3. She never drinks *coffee / coffees* after 9 pm.
4. What's your favorite *pizza / pizzas*?
5. Can you buy some *bread / breads* on your way home?
6. Is there *an onion / onions* in this recipe?

B Complete the sentences with *some, any, a* or *an*.

1. Did you buy ______________ carrots at the grocery store?
2. Are there ______________ good restaurants near here?
3. Would you like ______________ more tea?
4. There's ______________ pasta in the cupboard.
5. Do you want ______________ orange?
6. There's ______________ bottle of water in the fridge.

➤ Go back to page 72.

8.2 *much, many, a lot of*

A Complete the paragraph with *a lot of, much* or *many*.

Although we're not vegetarians, we eat [1]______________ vegetables. I like tomatoes, but there aren't [2]______________ in our local market at the moment because it's winter. At breakfast we usually have cereal and [3]______________ fruit. Fresh fruit is really good for you. We don't eat [4]______________ meat, but we sometimes have chicken on Sundays. My son loves potatoes so we always have [5]______________ potatoes with our Sunday dinner. We all like a delicious dessert, but we don't eat [6]______________ chocolate.

B Complete the sentences with *much* or *many*.

1. How ___much___ money do you have?
2. How ___________ people are coming to dinner?
3. How ___________ water do you drink every day?
4. How ___________ do you spend on food every month?
5. How ___________ sugar do you want in your coffee?
6. How ___________ bottles of water do we need?
7. How ___________ packages of cookies do you have?

➤ Go back to page 75.

8.3 *a/an, the*, no article

A Choose the correct options to complete the paragraph.

Levain Bakery is [1]*the / a / an* company that makes [2]*the / – / an* chocolate cookies. [3]*The / A / –* company is in [4]*the / a / –* New York, but it sells cookies all across [5]*the / a / an* US.

B Complete the paragraphs with *the, a, an* or –.

[1]________ Jamie Oliver is [2]________ English chef who is famous in [3]________ UK and across [4]________ world. He has a lot of restaurants and [5]________ popular TV shows. [6]________ People love cooking and eating his Italian recipes.

[7]________ Wellington Froots is [8]________ company that grows and delivers fresh [9]________ fruits and vegetables. Friends Isabella Sheridan and Akiko Okamura started their business in Isabella's home city of [10]________ Wellington, in [11]________ New Zealand. [12]________ company delivers [13]________ new box of locally grown, fresh ingredients to its customers every week.

C Correct the mistakes in each sentence.

1. My dad has an great recipe for carrot cake!
2. Let's go to a new French restaurant on Broad Street.
3. Ramen is a popular noodle dish from the Sapporo, Japan.
4. Could you get me a grater? It's in that cupboard over there.
5. The junk food is bad for your health.
6. Could you buy the onion on your way home? I need one for this recipe.

➤ Go back to page 76.

Grammar Hub

9.1 Present progressive

	Positive	Negative
I	**I'm talking** to my friend.	**I'm not feeling** very well.
he/she/it	**She's wearing** shorts and a t-shirt.	**She isn't working** today.
you/we/they	**They're playing** cards.	**They aren't wearing** uniforms.

	Question	Short answers	
I	**Am I saying** it correctly?	Yes, **you are**.	No, **you aren't**.
he/she/it	**Is she wearing** a backpack?	Yes, **she is**.	No, **she isn't**.
you/we/they	**Are you doing** it together?	Yes, **we are**.	No, **we aren't**.

Spelling rules	base form	*-ing*
Add **-ing**.	look	look**ing**
Drop the **-e** with verbs ending **-e**.	give	giv**ing**
Double the final consonant with verbs ending consonant, vowel, consonant + **-ing**.	sto**p**	sto**pping**

- We use the present progressive to talk about things happening now.
- In the negative, with *you*, *he*, etc we can also say: *You're not + -ing, He's not + -ing, She's not + -ing, It's not + -ing, We're not + -ing, They're not + -ing.*

  *It **isn't** raining. OR **It's not** raining.*
- In negative short answers, with *you*, *he*, etc we can also say: *No, you're not., No, he's not., No, she's not., No, it's not., No, we're not., No, they're not.*

  *Are they driving to work at the moment? No, **they aren't**. OR No, **they're not**.*

9.2 Simple present vs present progressive

- We use the simple present to talk about habits and routines.

  *He **wears** a suit to work **every day**.*
- We also use the simple present to talk about things that are true in general.

  *They **usually dress up** for a party.*
- We use the present progressive to talk about things happening now.

  *Take a coat – **it's raining** outside.*
- We also use the present progressive to talk about things happening around now.

  ***I'm working** in Berlin for a month. I usually work in New York.*

Be careful!

- We often use the simple present with the time expressions *all day*, *every week*, *once a year*, and adverbs like *always*, *often*, *usually* and *never*.
- We often use the present progressive with the time expressions *(right) now* and *at the moment*.

9.3 Object pronouns

Subject pronoun	Object pronoun
I	me
he	him
she	her
it	it
we	us
you	you
they	them

- We use object pronouns after a verb or after a preposition.

  After a verb: *Can you **show me** a different dress, please?*
- After a preposition: *It's Dinu's birthday. I'm buying a present **for her**.*

9.1 Present progressive

A Complete the conversations with the present progressive form of the verbs in parentheses. Use contractions where possible.

1 A: Where are you?
B: We ______________ (get) off the bus right now.

2 A: ______________ he ______________ (come) now?
B: Yes, very soon.

3 A: Where's Ahmed?
B: He ______________ (have) lunch.

4 A: Are you at work?
B: No, I ______________ (sit) in the park.

5 A: What ______________ you ______________ (read) at the moment?
B: *The Secret History* by Donna Tartt. It's amazing!

6 A: What are you up to?
B: I ______________ (watch) the rugby game.

B Use the prompts to complete the text messages. Use contractions where possible.

What ___are you doing___ (you / do) now?

1 ______________ (I / watch) TV. What about you?

2 ______________ (I / walk) the dog.
3 ______________ (she / wear) her new collar. Is Elle with you?

No, she isn't here. She's with Wes. 4 ______________ (they / go) to the gym now.

5 ______________ (you / go) too?

No, I'm too tired.

➤ Go back to page 83.

9.2 Simple present vs present progressive

A Choose the correct option.

1 The department store ***opens / is opening*** at nine o'clock every day.
2 I ***don't usually give / am not usually giving*** fashion advice.
3 He ***wears / 's wearing*** a Hugo Boss suit and Prada shoes.
4 It looks like she ***enjoys / 's enjoying*** the fashion show.
5 In the US, students usually ***don't wear / aren't wearing*** a uniform to school.
6 Today, I ***work / 'm working*** on a report for Gemma.
7 It usually ***snows / is snowing*** at this time of year.
8 I can't meet tomorrow. I ***work / 'm working*** from home on Tuesdays.

B Complete the conversations with the simple present or present progressive forms of the verbs in parentheses.

1 A: Can ______________ (I / speak) to Rosanna Francis?
B: Sorry, ______________ (she / not / be) here. Can I take a message?

2 A: Hey! Where ______________ (you /be)?
B: ______________ (I / leave) now.

3 A: ______________ (you / watch) the news?
B: No. Why? What ______________ (be / happen)?

4 A: Where ______________ (be / you / from)?
B: I ______________ (be / from) a small town in northern Spain.

5 A: What ______________ (you / cook)?
B: I ______________ (be / make) spaghetti.

➤ Go back to page 85.

9.3 Object pronouns

A Complete the sentences with the object pronouns in the box.

me	you	him	her	it	them

1 My sister loves clothes. I always go shopping with ______________.
2 I love blue. It's the best color for ______________.
3 Alison loves shoes. She spends a lot of money on ______________.
4 Tom's very friendly. His customers like ______________.
5 Jin want's a new cell phone. She's saving up for ______________.
6 I bought ______________ a cup of coffee, Doug. Be careful – it's hot!

B Complete the sentences with subject or object pronouns.

1 I need some new clothes, but ______________ don't want to spend a lot of money on ______________.
2 My sister gives great fashion advice. ______________ always enjoy clothes shopping with ______________.
3 Daniel doesn't have a lot of money, so ______________ don't think ______________ can afford those shoes.
4 I follow Mark Greenwood on Instagram. ______________'s a fashion blogger.
5 Jo has three sisters. ______________ always borrowed each other's clothes when ______________ were younger!

➤ Go back to page 87.

Grammar Hub

10.1 Comparatives

		Adjective	Comparative
One syllable	Add **-er**.	high	higher
More than one syllable	Add **more** + adjective.	beautiful	more beautiful
Irregular	Use irregular comparative.	good	better
		bad	worse
		far	farther

Spelling rules		
Add **-er**.	cheap	cheap**er**
Add **-r** with adjectives that end in **-e**.	larg**e**	large**r**
Double the consonant and add **-er** with adjectives that end vowel + consonant.	ho**t**	ho**tter**

- We use comparatives to say how two or more things are different.

  *Mount Everest is **higher** than Ben Nevis.*
  *Thailand is **more beautiful** than Alaska.*
- Some two-syllable adjectives can form one-word comparatives.

  dirty → dirtier *quiet → quieter*
  narrow → narrower
- Comparatives are often followed by *than* but not always.

  *Avatar was better **than** The Beach. OR The Beach was good but Avatar was better.*

10.2 Superlatives

		Adjective	Superlative
One syllable	Add **the** + **-est**.	cold	the coldest
More than one syllable	Add **the most** + adjective.	remote	the most remote
Irregular	Use **the** + irregular superlative.	good	the best
		bad	the worst
		far	the farthest

Spelling rules		
Add **-est**.	cheap	cheap**est**
Add **-st** with adjectives that end in **-e**.	larg**e**	large**st**
Double the consonant and add **-est** with adjectives that end vowel + consonant.	ho**t**	ho**ttest**

- We use superlatives to say that something is top or bottom of a group.

  *The Atacama is **the coldest** dry desert in the world.*
  *What's **the most** remote place in your country?*
- Some two-syllable adjectives can form superlatives without *most*.

  dirty → the dirtiest *quiet → the quietest*
  narrow → the narrowest
- We often put *the* before superlatives but not always.

  Megan is my best friend. NOT ~~Megan is my the best friend.~~
  *Megan is **the best** friend I've ever had.*

10.3 Verb + *to* + infinitive

	verb + infinitive
decide	We **decided to go** hiking in the mountains.
forget	Don't **forget to take** your cell phone.
help	The map **helped** us **to find** the way.
learn	They're **learning to use** a compass.
need	You **need to build** a place to sleep.
plan	I'm **planning to hike** through the jungle next summer.
prefer	She **prefers to travel** by car.
remember	**Remember to set off** early.
try	She's **trying to start** a fire.
want	I **want to know** more about survival.

- Many verbs are followed by the infinitive.

Be careful!

*I plan **to go** to Rome next summer.*
NOT ~~I plan going to Rome next summer.~~
NOT ~~I plan go to Rome next summer.~~

10.1 Comparatives

A Write the comparative form of each adjective.

1 old ____*older*____
2 big ________
3 dirty ________
4 expensive ________
5 bad ________

B Match to make sentences.

1 Moscow is colder than
2 December is hotter
3 The city is more
4 Riding a motorcycle is more
5 Is Romania more
6 The Burj Khalifa is taller

a crowded than the countryside.
b New York.
c beautiful than Ireland?
d than the Eiffel Tower.
e dangerous than driving a car.
f than July.

C Correct the mistakes in each sentence.

1 The mountains are ~~more cold~~ *colder* than the desert.
2 Mount Everest is biger than Mount Kilimanjaro.
3 K2 is the more dangerous than Mount Everest.
4 The Nile is more long than the Amazon.
5 It's difficulter to film in the jungle than in a city.
6 The UK is bigger as Ireland.
7 Ireland is famouser for mountains than beaches.

➤ Go back to page 93.

10.2 Superlatives

A Write the superlative form of each adjective.

1 tall ____*the tallest*____
2 hot ________
3 sunny ________
4 beautiful ________
5 good ________

B Choose the correct options to complete the sentences.

1 Aconcagua is the *most tall / tallest* mountain in South America.
2 The Pacific is the *most big / biggest* ocean in the world.
3 I think the Newfoundland is the *most beautiful / beautifullest* dog in the world!
4 Mawsynram is the *most wet / wettest* place on Earth.
5 Hanoi is the *most ancient / ancientest* city in Vietnam.
6 Parinacota is the *most high / highest* city in Chile.

C Complete the sentences with the correct superlative form of the adjective in parentheses. Add *the*.

1 Yakutsk is ________ (cold) city in the world.
2 Is Monaco ________ (expensive) country to live in?
3 Death Valley is ________ (hot) place on Earth.
4 Tristan Da Cunha is ________ (remote) island on the planet.
5 The Tata Nano is ________ (cheap) car in the world.
6 Valletta is ________ (sunny) place in Europe.

➤ Go back to page 95.

10.3 Verb + infinitive

A Complete the sentences with *to* and the verbs in the box.

bring (x2) carry go make read travel

1 I forgot ____*to bring*____ my raincoat with me.
2 I'm trying ________ the map, but it's really dark.
3 They should get some wood. They need ________ a fire to keep warm.
4 Did you remember ________ a bottle of water with you?
5 She's planning ________ to Greece for a vacation next year.
6 We helped ________ the boxes into the house.
7 I don't like flying – I prefer ________ by train.

B Reorder the words to make sentences. Add *to* in the right place.

1 you / need / boil the water / don't
You don't need to boil the water.
2 for / they / decided / go / a / walk
____
3 planning / we're / the / world / travel
____
4 before dark / get / hope / there / we
____
5 needs / some camping equipment / she / buy
____
6 in the jungle / must learn / they / survive
____
7 do / a survival course / I / don't want
____

➤ Go back to page 97.

Grammar Hub

11.1 *should* and *shouldn't*

	Positive	Negative	
I/you/we/they	**You should drink** lots of water.	**You shouldn't smoke**.	
	Question	Short answers	
he/she/it	**Should I buy** a return ticket?	Yes, **you should**.	No, **you shouldn't**.

- We use *should* to give advice.
- We use *should/shouldn't* + base form.

Be careful!

You should rest. NOT ~~*You should to rest.*~~ NOT ~~*You should resting.*~~

11.2 Present perfect

	Positive	Negative
I/you/we/they	**I've climbed** Mount Everest.	We **haven't visited** the Burj Khalifa.
he/she/it	**She's ridden** an elephant.	He **hasn't been** to Africa.

	Question	Short answers	
I/you/we/they	**Have you (ever) been** to New York?	Yes, **we have**.	No, **we haven't**.
he/she/it	**Has she (ever) eaten** sushi?	Yes, **she has**.	No, **she hasn't**.

- We use the present perfect to talk about past experiences.
- We use *have/has* + past participle.
- With the present perfect, we don't say when the action happened.

  I've ridden a motorcycle. NOT ~~*I've ridden a motorcycle yesterday.*~~
- We can use *ever* in questions to mean 'before now'.
- We can use *never* in negative statements.

  *I've **never** jumped out of an airplane.*

Be careful!

- We use *been* not *gone* to talk about places we have visited.

  *I have never **been** to China.* NOT ~~*I have never gone to China.*~~
- Be careful with the past participles of common irregular verbs.

  bring → brought *buy → bought* *do → done*
  go → gone/been *make → made* *think → thought*
  write → written

See **Irregular Verbs** on **page IV** for more information.

11.3 Present perfect vs simple past

- We use the present perfect to talk about an action in the past, but we don't say when it happened.

  *Yes, I've **been** to Canada.* NOT ~~*Yes, I've been to Canada in 2015.*~~
- We use the simple past to talk about an action at a specific time in the past.

  *She went to Greece **in 2016**.* NOT ~~*She has been to Greece in 2016.*~~
- We use time expressions with the simple past, *not* the present perfect.

  *I went to Hawaii three years **ago**.* NOT ~~*I've been to Hawaii three years ago.*~~

  *We took the train to work **yesterday**.* NOT ~~*We've taken the train to work yesterday.*~~

Be careful!

- We often ask a general question about past experiences using the present perfect.
- Then we use the simple past to ask for or give more details.

  A: Have you ever been to France?
  B: Yes, I have.
  A: When did you go?
  B: Two years ago.

11.1 *should* and *shouldn't*

A Complete the sentences with *should* or *shouldn't*.

1 That's a bad cough. You really ______________ see a doctor.

2 You ______________ smoke – it's really bad for your health.

3 If you want to lose weight, you ______________ exercise more.

4 If you're sick, you ______________ go to work today. You could make other people sick.

5 You look really tired. You ______________ go to bed early.

6 A: ______________ I take my medicine now?
B: Yes, you ______________.

B Use the prompts to write sentences with *should* or *shouldn't*.

1 *You shouldn't eat* (you / not / eat) late at night.

2 ______________ (we / not / listen) to loud music.

3 ______________ (I / go) to the gym more often?

4 When ______________ (I / take) my medicine?

5 ______________ (she / not / have) four coffees every day.

6 ______________ (they / drink) lots of water.

7 ______________ (he / not / watch) so much TV.

➤ Go back to page 103.

11.2 Present perfect

A Complete the sentences with the past participle form of the verbs in the box.

~~appear~~ climb do forget been visit

1 I've *appeared* on a TV show twice.

2 Have you ever ______________ a mountain?

3 She's never ______________ her first airplane jump.

4 They haven't ______________ any dangerous activities.

5 We have ______________ Korea three times.

6 Have you ever ______________ to Greece?

B Complete the sentences with the present perfect form of the verb in parentheses. Use contractions where possible.

1 He ______________ (not play) any sports in his life.

2 They ______________ (never go) to Iceland.

3 We ______________ (swim) in the Mediterranean Sea.

4 ______________ (you ever drive) a sports car?

5 I ______________ (meet) Taylor Swift.

6 She ______________ (never play) tennis on grass.

➤ Go back to page 105.

11.3 Present perfect vs simple past

A Choose the correct tense to complete the sentences.

1 She*'s been / went* to Denmark last year.

2 They*'ve traveled / traveled* to Chile a long time ago.

3 *Have you biked / Did you bike* to work yesterday?

4 *Have you ever been / Did you ever go* to Vietnam?

5 We*'ve driven / drove* across Europe last summer.

6 *Have you tried / Did you try* snowboarding when you were in Switzerland?

B Complete the text messages with the present perfect or simple past form of the verb in parentheses.

Virginia: [1] ______________ (go) skiing last week?

Teresa: Yes, we [2] ______________. [3] ______________ (ever go) skiing?

Virginia: No, I [4] ______________. I [5] ______________ (do) any winter sports.

Teresa: Really? I [6] ______________ (try) both skiing and snowboarding. They're really fun!

➤ Go back to page 107.

Grammar Hub

12.1 *going to*

	Positive	Negative
I	**I'm going to travel** around Japan after college.	**I'm not going to work** in an office when I graduate.
he/she/it	**She's going to book** the tickets next week.	**She isn't going to visit** Kyoto during her trip.
you/we/they	**We're going to stay** in hostels.	**We aren't going to book** anything until we get there.

	Question	Short answers	
I	**Am I going to get** in trouble for this?	Yes, **you are**.	No, **you aren't**.
he/she/it	**Is he going to make** a reservation for both of us?	Yes, **he is**.	No, **he isn't**.
you/we/they	**Are you going to speak** to her next week?	Yes, **we are**.	No, **we aren't**.

- We use *going to* to talk about future plans and intentions.
- In the negative, with *you*, *he*, etc, we can also say: *You're not going to*, *He's not going to*, etc.

  *She **isn't** going to book anything until next month.* OR *She's **not** going to book anything until next month.*
- In negative short answers, with *you*, *he*, etc, we can also say: *No, you're not.*, *No, he's not.*, etc.

  *Are they going to visit the Guggenheim? No, **they aren't**.* OR *No, **they're not**.*

12.2 *will* for predictions

	Positive	Negative
I/you/he/she/it/we/they	Rock music **will be** popular forever.	Students **won't go** to school in the future.

	Question	Short answers	
I/you/he/she/it/we/they	**Will they visit** Mars in our lifetime?	Yes, **they will**.	No, **they won't**.

- We use *will* + base form to make predictions.

  Germany will win the next World Cup.

  In 10 years' time, most people will drive electric cars.
- In the positive, we often contract *will* to *'ll* in informal writing and speech.
- In the negative, we can also say *will not*. This is more formal.

  *Schools **will not** teach the same subjects in the future.*

Be careful!

- We often use *will* after *Do you think* … .

  *Do you think the party **will** be fun?*

12.3 *might*

	Positive	Negative
I/you/he/she/it/we/they	**I might stop** using Facebook.	**She might not read** my tweets.

- We use *might* to talk about something that is not definite but possible.
- We use *might* + base form.

12.1 *going to*

A Reorder the words to make sentences.

1 go / going to / backpacking around Europe / she's
She's going to go backpacking around Europe.
2 study / at a university / going to / I'm / art history
______
3 going to / the tickets / when / are you / book / ?
______
4 a new job / start / I'm / looking for / going to
______
5 build / they're / themselves / going to / it
______

B Complete the sentences with the correct form of *be going to* and the verbs in parentheses. Use contractions where possible.

1 *Are you going to have* (you / have) a big birthday party?
2 ______ (she / finish) her essay this weekend.
3 When ______ (they / travel) to Bucharest?
4 What time ______ (you / get up) tomorrow?
5 ______ (it / not / be) cold tonight.
6 ______ (we / not / arrive) until late.

➤ Go back to page 112.

12.2 *will* for predictions

A Reorder the words to make sentences.

In the year 2025

1 there / flying / cars / be / will
______
2 won't / be / school / there / books / any
______
3 cities / other / have / planets / on / we'll
______
4 robots / do / work / all / the / will / us / for
______
5 come / true / will / our / predictions / all
______
6 with / people / will / around / jetpacks / fly
______

B Use the prompts to write questions and short answers with *will*.

1 we / finish / on time?
Will we finish on time? (?) *Yes, we will.* (+)
2 she / read / your diary
______ (?) ______ (+)
3 you / work and study / at the same time
______ (?) ______ ( )
4 his predictions / come true
______ (?) ______ (-)
5 he / get / a better job
______ (?) ______ (+)
6 Chris / be / at the party
______ (?) ______ (-)

➤ Go back to page 115.

12.3 *might*

A Complete the sentences with *might* or *might not*.

1 I ______ be able to come on Saturday, because I have to help my friend move.
2 Do you want me to give Tom a message? I ______ see him at the conference.
3 I'll try, but I ______ be able to get everything finished in time.
4 I ______ be home late tonight because I have lots of work to finish.
5 You should call Sarah. She ______ think you've forgotten her!

B Complete the sentences with the correct form of *might* and a verb in the box.

go take have ~~see~~ send wait

1 OK, great. I *might see* you later then.
2 You're right. I ______ her an email to check the flight time.
3 It's hot in here. I ______ outside.
4 I ______ the bus, because it's cheaper than a taxi.
5 She ______ time to finish everything.
6 I ______ tonight. I'm not feeling very well.

➤ Go back to page 117.

Vocabulary Hub

7.1 Transportation

Match pictures (1–12) with the words in the box.

___ bicycle ___ boat ___ bus ___ car ___ ferry ___ motorcycle
___ plane ___ cruise ship ___ taxi ___ train ___ trolley ___ subway

➤ Go back to page 62.

7.2 Travel phrases

Complete the email using the past tense of the verbs in the box.

arrive leave miss return take

To: Samantha

Dear Samantha,

We're back! We visited my parents last week. Our journey home was terrible. It took a long time. We [1] ______________ my parents' house on Saturday evening. We [2] ______________ a bus and then a train to Caracas. We [3] ______________ in the city at lunchtime on Sunday. Unfortunately, the traffic on the way to the airport was really bad, and we [4] ______________ our flight! So we [5] ______________ to the city and stayed in a hotel. In the end, we got home on Wednesday, four days after leaving my parents' house!

Talk to you later.

Rose

➤ Go back to page 65.

8.1 Food and drink

A Label the images (1–15) with the words in the box.

an apple butter cake cheese chicken chips eggs lettuce mushrooms pasta potatoes shrimp rice tea tomatoes

1  ________

2  ________

3  ________

4  ________

5  ________

6  ________

7  ________

8  ________

9  ________

10  ________

11  ________

12  ________

13  ________

14  ________

15  ________

B Complete the table with words from Exercise A.

Dairy	
Meat and fish	
Fruits and vegetables	
Drinks	
Other	

➤ Go back to page 72.

8.2 Containers

Complete the labels (1–8) with words from the box.

a bag a bottle a box a carton a jar a package a container a can

1 ________ of water

5 ________ of yogurt

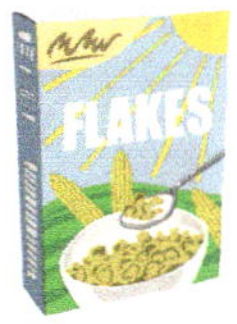

2 ________ of cereal

6 ________ of rice

3 ________ of milk

7 ________ of beans

4 ________ of cookies

8 ________ of jam

➤ Go back to page 75.

Vocabulary Hub

9.1 Clothes

A Match pictures (1–18) with the words in the box.

___ boots ___ coat ___ dress ___ gloves ___ hat
___ headscarf ___ sweater ___ scarf ___ shirt
___ shoes ___ shorts ___ skirt ___ socks ___ sunglasses
___ T-shirt ___ tie ___ sneakers ___ pants

1 
2 
3 
4 
5 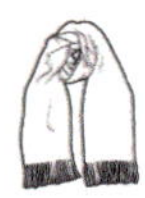
6 
7 
8 
9 
10 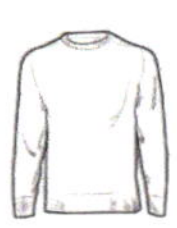
11 
12 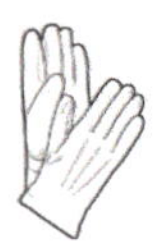
13 
14 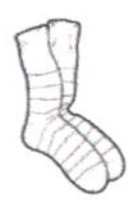
15 
16 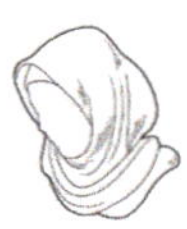
17 
18 

B Complete the descriptions with words from Exercise A.

I like Nobel Peace Prize winner Malala Yousafzai's style. It's traditional and beautiful. She usually wears a [1] ______________, a long [2] ______________, a pair of [3] ______________ and some simple shoes.

I prefer simple styles, like Mark Zuckerberg's. He usually wears a [4] ______________, a pair of blue jeans and a pair of sporty [5] ______________.

Emma Watson is so stylish. She looks great when she wears a black [6] ______________ and a pair of black [7] ______________.

➤ Go back to page 82.

9.3 Stores and services

Match the words in the box with pictures (1–12).

___ bakery ___ bank ___ bookstore ___ butcher's ___ department store ___ dentist's
___ hairdresser's ___ library ___ market ___ newsstand ___ pharmacy ___ grocery store

1 
2 
3 
4 
5 
6 
7 
8 
9 
10 
11 
12 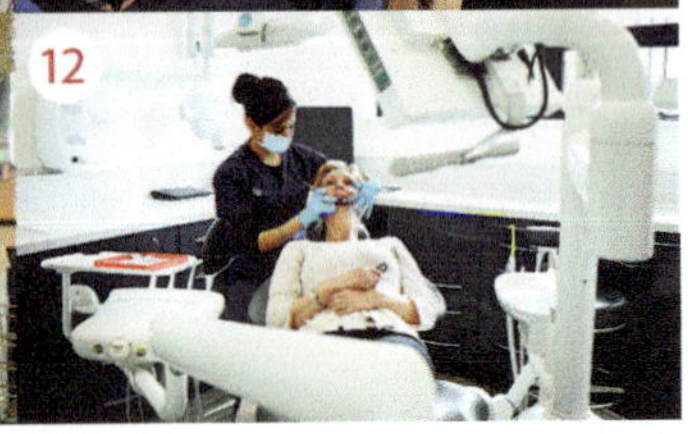

➤ Go back to page 87.

10.2 Seasons and weather

A Label the images with the words in the box.

fall spring summer winter

B Match phrases (1–8) with pictures (a–h). Some phrases can go with more than one picture.

1 It's cloudy. ___
2 It's cold. ___
3 It's foggy. ___
4 It's hot. ___
5 It's raining. ___
6 It's snowing. ___
7 It's sunny. ___
8 It's windy. ___

➤ Go back to page 95.

10.3 Phrasal verbs

Choose the correct phrasal verbs to complete the text.

Around two years ago, my husband and I went hiking in Austria. When we [1]***set off*** / ***gave up***, it was fairly cold, but then it got hotter and I [2]***put on*** / ***took off*** my jacket. The mountain air felt so nice! We walked for a really long time. In fact, we got lost! We [3]***found out*** / ***looked for*** our car, but we couldn't find it. We met a man and we tried to talk to him. We wanted to [4]***find out*** / ***look for*** where the nearest village was, but he didn't understand us. In the evening, it got really cold. I [5]***put on*** / ***took off*** my jacket, but it wasn't enough. We were frightened and we were ready to [6]***set off*** / ***give up***, but then we found a village! The police officer told us that our car was only a three minute walk from the police station!

➤ Go back to page 97.

Vocabulary Hub

11.2 Irregular past participles

Complete the sentences with the past participle form of the verbs in the box. There are two verbs you do not need.

be do go have ride see take win

1 I've never ________________ a horse and I don't want to.
2 She's ________________ three running races.
3 I've ________________ to more than ten countries.
4 They've ________________ the sun rise in Africa.
5 I've never ________________ a meal that cost more than $100.
6 He's ________________ a picture of a famous person.

➤ Go back to page 105.

11.3 Sports

A Label the pictures with the words in the box.

badminton basketball bike riding golf gymnastics judo ice skating skiing surfing ~~swimming~~ tennis yoga

1 *swimming*

2 ________________

3 ________________

4 ________________

5 ________________

6 ________________

7 ________________

8 ________________

9 ________________

10 ________________

11 ________________

12 ________________

B Match the sports in Exercise A with the correct verb – *do*, *go* or *play*.

Play	________________ ________________ ________________ ________________
Do	________________ ________________ ________________
Go	________________ ________________ ________________ ________________ ________________

➤ Go back to page 107.

12.2 Collocations with *get*

A Write the phrases with *get* in the correct place.

get home get hot get lunch get some coffee get there get tired

Become	Buy or obtain	Arrive

B Think of two more phrases for each meaning of *get*. Add them to Exercise A.

➤ Go back to page 115.

10.2 Student A

A Use the prompts to make superlative questions.

1 small / city / in the world?
2 hot / city / in Europe?
3 wet / place / on Earth?
4 high / city / in South America?
5 old / city / in Africa?
6 remote / city / in the world?
7 big / jungle / in the world?

B **SPEAK** Ask Student B your questions and write down the answers. Answer Student B's questions using the information box below.

Tokyo, Japan – 37 million people
Argos, Greece – 6th century BC
Winnipeg, Canada – minus 45°C (1966)
El Azizia, Libya – 58°C
Lhasa, Tibet – 3,600 m
Singapore
The Sahara Desert – 9 million km^2

A: What's the biggest city in the world?
B: The biggest city in the world is Tokyo, Japan. Thirty-seven million people live there.

➤ Go back to page 95.

8.1 Student A

Look at the picture. Ask Student B what's in their fridge. Answer Student B's questions. What is the same? What is different?

➤ Go back to page 73.

12.3 Student A and B

A **SPEAK** Interview your classmates about how they use social media. Write notes. Ask for more information.

SOCIAL MEDIA HABITS

1 Which social network do you use the most?
a Facebook b Twitter
c LinkedIn d other

2 How often do you 'like' things?
a fewer than 5 times a day
b 5–10 times a day
c 11–20 times a day
d more than 20 times a day

3 What do you share the most?
a pictures b videos
c news stories d funny stories

4 How many people do you follow?
a fewer than 50 b 50–100
c 101–300 d more than 300

5 How often do you chat?
a fewer than 5 times a day
b 5–10 times a day
c 11–20 times a day
d more than 20 times a day

6 In the future, how much do you think you'll use social media?
a more b less
c the same amount d not at all

B **ORGANIZE** Work in groups. Compare your answers. Organize them into statistics.

Most people share news stories.
Nobody tweets every day.

➤ Go back to page 117.

12.1 Student A

Look at Andrew's list of five things he has to do. Ask and answer questions to find the missing information.

A: What's Andrew going to do on Friday?
B: He's going to …

1 This afternoon – call James Smith.
2 ______________ on Friday.
3 Send out the conference invitations next week.
4 Tomorrow morning – ______________.
5 Today – ______________!

➤ Go back to page 113.

7.2 Student A and B

Work in pairs. Follow these instructions to play the game:

- Use a dice and counters to play the board game.
- Complete the sentences with the simple past form of the verbs in parentheses.
- Every time you get the answer right, roll again!

25 SPIN AGAIN!	**26** They (not take) the train to Spain; they (go) by bus.	**27** You missed the train. Go back to **6**.	**28** I (not see) the Colosseum when I (be) in Rome.	**FINISH**
24 There's a storm. Go back to **8**.	**23** I (go) to Thailand last year.	**22** We (not fly) to Mexico; we sailed.	**21** You're in a traffic jam. Go back to **12**.	**20** SPIN AGAIN!
15 We (not book) a hotel; we (stay) with friends.	**16** You forgot your passport. Go to **3**.	**17** SPIN AGAIN!	**18** We (not go) to Malaysia by train; we (go) by car.	**19** They (take) the ferry.
14 He (not go) to Rome.	**13** He (miss) the train.	**12** You only have a carry-on bag. Go to **18**.	**11** SPIN AGAIN!	**10** They (not arrive) in Bogotá until 5 am.
5 SPIN AGAIN!	**6** They (not take) much luggage.	**7** They (miss) their flight to France.	**8** She (leave) at 8 am.	**9** Your flight arrived 30 minutes early. Go to **18**.
4 SPIN AGAIN!	**3** I (travel) to Dubai by plane.	**2** You have a first-class ticket. Go to **8**.	**1** She (take) a train to London.	**START**

➤ Go back to page 65.

7.3 Student A and B

SPEAK Work in pairs. Use the pictures to tell the story of Max and Sarah's vacation.

➤ Go back to page 67.

12.1 Student B

Look at Andrew's list of five things he has to do. Ask and answer questions to find the missing information.

A: What's Andrew going to do this afternoon?
B: He's going to …

1 This afternoon – ____________________.
2 Email the design company on Friday.
3 ____________________ next week.
4 Tomorrow morning – arrange a meeting with Max.
5 Today – write the PRS report!

➤ Go back to page 113.

8.1 Student B

Look at the picture. Ask Student A what's in their fridge. Answer Student A's questions. What is the same? What is different?

➤ Go back to page 73.

10.2 Student B

A Use the prompts to make superlative questions.

1 big / city / in the world?
2 old / city / in Europe?
3 cold / city / in North America?
4 hot / place / in the world?
5 high / city / in Asia?
6 expensive / city / in the world?
7 big / desert / in the world?

B SPEAK Ask Student A your questions and write down the answers. Answer Student A's questions using the information box below.

Vatican City, Rome – 800 people
Athens – 22°C average temperature in summer
Mawsynram, India – 11,871 mm of rain every year
La Rinconada, Peru – 5,101 m
Luxor, Egypt – 3200 BC
Auckland, New Zealand – 2,153 km from Sydney
The Amazon rainforest – 5.5 million km^2

A: What's the smallest city in the world?
B: The smallest city in the world is the Vatican City in Rome. Eight hundred people live there.

➤ Go back to page 95.

9.2 Student A and B

A You are going to interview your partner about their job/studies. Write questions using the prompts (1–7).

1 What / do?
2 Where / (work/study)?
3 What / do / every day?
4 What / enjoy / about / (job/course)? What / not enjoy?
5 Where / live / at the moment?
6 What / interest / in?
7 What / do / today?

B SPEAK Interview your partner using the questions from Exercise A. Write notes.

C SPEAK Work in small groups. Imagine two students in the class are going to swap jobs for a day. Use your notes from Exercise B to help you choose which students should swap jobs. Explain why.

Fumi is interested in art and Alex works in a museum. Maybe they should swap jobs.

Good idea!

➤ Go back to page 85.

10.3 Student A and B

A Work in pairs. Which of the following places do you think is the most difficult to survive in? Why?

a forest   an island   a jungle   a mountain

B PLAN Work in pairs. Imagine you are lost in one of the places in Exercise A. What are the dangers? What can help you? Choose three items to take with you.

Location	
Dangers	
Things to take	

C ORGANIZE Write a survival plan.

SURVIVAL PLAN
We can use the pocketknife to cut up fruit.
We can use the matches to light a fire – wild animals won't like the fire!

D PRESENT Tell the class your ideas.

➤ Go back to page 97.

Write a short article about a travel experience

W *so* and *because*

A Work in pairs. What makes a vacation good or bad?

B Read *Travel spotlight: Tulum*. Which of the things you discussed in Exercise A are mentioned?

Travel spotlight: TULUM

Last month, I traveled to Tulum, in Mexico. It's fairly easy to get there. I flew to Cancún, and then took a bus. I wanted to be near the ocean, so I stayed in a small hotel on the beach. It was really beautiful. For three days, I read books and swam in the clear, blue ocean.

Tulum is a small town, but there are lots of things to do, so it isn't boring! During the day, you can visit historic places near the beach or go kite surfing. You can also visit the Sian Ka'an nature park and see birds, animals and fish. I went on a day trip to Chichen Itza because I like history.

At night, you can eat dinner in one of the great restaurants in town, or you can go salsa dancing in a club. The food at the hotel was really good – I ate fresh fish every day!

Tulum is a great place for a nice beach vacation with some interesting places to visit. A return flight to Cancún costs around $500. The best time of year to go to Tulum is between December and April because it's sunny, but not too hot.

C Read again and answer the questions.

1 Where did the writer go? ______
2 How did she travel there? ______
3 Where did she stay? ______
4 What did she do during the day? ______
5 What can you do at night? ______
6 What was the food like? ______
7 When is the best time to visit? ______

D Complete the sentences with *so* or *because*. Use the information in the box to help you.

> ***so* and *because***
>
> - We use *so* to talk about the result of something.
>   *I wanted to be near the ocean,* ***so*** *I stayed in a small hotel on the beach.*
>   *But there are lots of things to do,* ***so*** *it isn't boring!*
> - We use *because* to explain the reason for something.
>   *I went on a day trip to Chichen Itza* ***because*** *I like history.*
>   *The best time of year to go to Tulum is between December and April* ***because*** *it's sunny, but not too hot.*

1 The writer flew to Cancún ___*because*___ it's near Tulum.
2 She stayed in the hotel ______ it was on the beach.
3 She is interested in history, ______ she went to Chichen Itza.
4 She ate fish every day ______ it was really fresh.
5 It isn't too hot between December and April, ______ it's the best time of year to go.

WRITING

A PREPARE You are going to write a travel blog about a place that you know. Write notes about the place. Use the questions in Exercise C to help you.

B PLAN Add more information to your notes. Use the travel blog in Exercise B to help you.

C WRITE Write your article. Use *so* and *because*.

8 Writing

Write an online restaurant review

W pronoun referencing

A SPEAK Work in pairs. Answer the questions.

1 Do you like eating out?
2 How often do you eat out?
3 What's your favorite type of restaurant?
4 Do you ever write online reviews about restaurants you visit?

B Read the two restaurant reviews. Who didn't have a good time?

Posted on 1/3/19 at 10:32am

Primavera ★

We chose Primavera because **it** had amazing reviews and we love Italian food. When we arrived, the music was really loud. I called the waitress and asked **her** to turn **it** down. **She** just walked away! It wasn't much better when we ordered our food. When the appetizers arrived, my fish wasn't cooked so I sent **it** back. My boyfriend said there was too much garlic on **his** shrimp – he didn't even finish **them**! For the main course, we had a salad and a steak. **They** were OK but nothing special. We didn't have a dessert. Overall, **it** cost too much and the food wasn't good. We didn't enjoy our meal and we won't go again.

Nor, Singapore

Share Like Comment

Posted on 3/17/19 at 3:25pm

Allium ★★★★

I wanted somewhere special for my wife's 30th birthday, so I chose the French restaurant, Allium. **It**'s very popular and so it wasn't easy to get a table. The piano player was really good and the service was great. There were fresh flowers on every table. **They** smelled wonderful. We ordered the soup and the mushrooms as appetizers. Then for the main course, I had the chicken and my wife had beef. We both had the lemon parfait for dessert. It was a fairly expensive meal, but the food was great so **it** was good value. Our waiter, Pascal, was really good, too, so we left **him** a big tip! We loved Allium. I really recommend **it** for a special occasion.

Dieter, Germany

Share Like Comment

C Read the reviews again and answer the questions. Choose Nor (N) or Dieter (D).

1	Who wasn't happy with the staff ?	N / D
2	Who thinks the food was good?	N / D
3	Who liked the music?	N / D
4	Who thinks their meal was too expensive?	N / D
5	Who doesn't recommend it?	N / D

D Complete the sentences with a pronoun. Use the information in the box to help you.

Pronoun referencing

The first time we talk about something, we use a noun. After that, we use pronouns to avoid repeating the noun and to make our writing flow.

*When we arrived, **the music** was really loud. I called **the waitress** and asked her to turn it down.*

1 We enjoyed our meal. ____ was delicious.
2 The waitress and the manager were unfriendly. ____ didn't help us at all.
3 The waiter only came to our table after I called ____ three times.
4 The appetizers were amazing. I can't recommend ____ highly enough.
5 My wife loved the restaurant. ____ wants to go back soon.
6 We liked our waitress and left ____ a good tip.

WRITING

A PREPARE Think about a good or bad experience you had at a restaurant. Write notes. Think about:

- who you were with
- the name of the restaurant
- what it looked like
- the type, choice and quality of the food
- the staff
- the cost

B WRITE Write a review of your restaurant. Use your notes from Exercise A to help you. Remember to use pronouns and to write about what you liked and didn't like.

C REVIEW Work in pairs. Read each other's reviews. Do you want to go to the restaurant your partner went to?

9 Writing

Write a social media post

W checking your work

A Work in pairs. Answer the questions.

1. What social media sites do you use?
2. Do you follow anyone on social media? Who?
3. Do you ever post pictures of yourself or friends/family on social media?
4. What kinds of pictures do people usually post on social media?

B Look at the pictures and read the social media posts. Match posts (a–d) with pictures (1–5). There is one picture you do not need.

C Read the posts again and answer the questions.

1. Why is the woman trying on sunglasses?
2. What are Daria and her friend looking for?
3. What are the people doing at the beach?
4. Why is the man having breakfast in a café?

D Find and correct two mistakes in each sentence. Use the information in the box to help you.

> **Checking your work**
>
> Always check your work for mistakes after you write something. Make sure you:
>
> - use the correct punctuation (capital letters, apostrophes, periods).
> - avoid common spelling mistakes, for example ~~fourty~~ *forty*.
> - use the correct grammar, for example, *I'm watching* ~~*watch*~~ *a movie at the moment.*

1. Were at the market and I eat an ice cream cone.
2. Like you thees shoes?
3. What you do at the moment?
4. I having a party beacause it's my birthday.

E Read post c again and correct:

- three punctuation mistakes
- three grammar mistakes
- three spelling mistakes

WRITING

A PREPARE Find a picture of yourself. (If you don't have one, imagine a picture that you want to describe.) Write notes about:

- where you are
- who you are with
- what you are doing

B WRITE Write a social media post about your picture. Use the posts in Exercise B to help you.

C REVIEW Check your work for mistakes. Use the strategies in the box to help you. Then swap with a partner and check their work.

a I'm having breakfast at my favorite café today. And I'm with my favorite person – my wife, Lucy! The eggs here at Kevin's are delicious. It's the perfect start to my birthday! ❤ #goodtimes

b We're at the market. I'm looking for some new sunglasses because it's really sunny here. What does everyone think of these? They're really funny! Everyone is looking at us! 😆 😆 #Spain

c Im spending the day with my best freind daria – we're shoping, obviously! I buyed a new top in a great little store. Now were looking for a place to have lunsh. Does anyone know a restaurant in Mango Grove that have good food. #bestfriends

d It's Saturday! Can you see where we are? That's right – at the beach! It's a beautiful day. The kids are eating ice cream cones. Rita's sleeping and I'm just relaxing! 😎

Share Like Comment

1

2

3

4

5

Write a product review

W – adverbs of manner

A Work in pairs. Look at the pictures. Answer the questions.

1 Do you own any of these items?
2 Where did you buy them?
3 Are they good quality?

1

a flashlight

2

a pocketknife

3

a backpack

4

a pair of walking boots

5

a tent

6
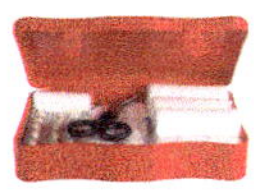
a first aid kit

7

a small camping stove

B Read three customer reviews. Which of the items in Exercise A are they for?

1 **I bought this to use at night on a camping trip.** I already have one, but this one is smaller and stronger. But it's also expensive and the batteries die very quickly. The most important thing is that it has a strong light! And it works really well, so I recommend it for beginner campers or hikers.

Published 1 week ago by Bob Smith

2 **I got this to use when I go fishing.** It's great and it does a lot of different things. It cuts nicely. It also has scissors and a can opener. Use it carefully, though. It can be dangerous! I'd recommend this to everyone!

Published 5 days ago by Greg Barnett

3 **I got this for our family vacation.** We understood the instructions easily, but it's too small. It says it's for four people, but I don't think that's true. It's also made very badly. And they have the worst customer service, too! After just one week, it broke, and now I can't get my money back. Don't buy this!

Published 2 days ago by Elizabeth Brown

C Which is a five-star (★★★★★) review, which is a three-star (★★★) review and which is a one-star (★) review? Why?

D Read the reviews again. Write notes about each using the table below.

	Review 1	Review 2	Review 3
What is the product?			
What are its bad points?			
What are its good points?			
Would the reviewer recommend it?			

E Find two adverbs of manner in each online review. Which adverb is irregular? Use the information in the box to help you.

Adverbs of manner

Adverbs of manner tell us how something happens.
It cuts nicely.
We add *-ly* to an adjective to make a regular adverb.
quick – quickly
For adjectives ending in *-y*, we drop the *-y* and add *-ily*.
easy – easily
Some adverbs are irregular.
hard – hard
good – well
Adverbs come after the main verb.
We understood the instructions easily.
Use it carefully.
We use words like *fairly*, *very* and *really* to add more information.
It's made very badly.
It works really well.

F Complete the sentences by making adverbs from the adjectives in parentheses.

1 The flashlight broke ________________ (*easy*).
2 The boots arrived very ________________ (*quick*).
3 Everything fits ________________ (*perfect*) into one bag.
4 The camping stove didn't work very ________________ (*good*).
5 Please use the pocketknife ________________ (*careful*) because it's very sharp.
6 The instructions say very ________________ (*clear*) there aren't any scissors in the first-aid kit.

WRITING

A PREPARE Imagine you have bought one of the items in Exercise A. Write down some good and bad things about it.

B WRITE Write a review of your product. Use the questions in Exercise D to help you. Use some adverbs of manner. Write about 50 words.

C REVIEW Work in pairs. Read each other's reviews. Can you find any mistakes? How many adverbs of manner can you find?

11 Writing

write a recommendation on a forum

W adding information with *too*, *also* and *as well*

A SPEAK Work in pairs. Do you ever give or read advice on chat forums? Which ones? What do you write about? Tell your partner.

B Work in pairs. Read the post on a fitness website. What sports or activities do you think Martin should try?

Martin | June 15, 4:17

Hi everyone. I'm 23 and I want to get fit. Can anyone recommend a sport or activity for me? I like doing things on my own and team sports, but I don't want to spend a lot of money. What should I try? Thanks!

C Read the replies to Martin's question. Do they match any of the things you thought of in Exercise B?

Luis | June 15, 4:25

Hi Martin! You should try yoga. It's really fun! You don't need any special equipment or clothes. One problem is that lessons are sometimes expensive. I found a yoga class in my town and I go twice a week. Now I can touch my toes!

Caitlin | June 15, 4:27

Hi there! I think you should try running. I've started a running club in my town. It's great! We go running together every week. Of course, you can also go running on your own. The best thing about running is that you can do it at any time you want! But be careful! Running is difficult, and it can hurt your knees as well. You should start slowly.

Marta | June 15, 4:27

What about soccer? I started five years ago and I love it. My friends and I play every week on a Saturday morning. Soccer is really good exercise, and it's fun, too! One problem is that you need to buy boots and sports clothes. You also need other people to play. You can't do it on your own. But I think it's more fun to exercise with friends!

D Read again and answer the questions. Write notes.

1 What sports and activities do the writers think Martin should try?

2 What good things do the writers say about the sports or activities?

3 What bad things do the writers talk about?

E Work in pairs. Whose advice do you think is best? Why?

Adding information with *too*, *also* and *as well*

We can use *too*, *also* and *as well* to add information to an idea.

Too and *as well* come at the end of the sentence.

Also comes before the main verb, but after the verb *be*.

F Work in pairs. Read again. Find and underline sentences with *also*, *too* and *as well*.

G Rewrite the second sentence using the word in parentheses. Use the Language information box to help you.

1 Golf is expensive. You need a lot of time. (also)

You also need a lot of time.

2 Swimming is good for your heart. It's good for your arms and legs. (as well)

____

3 You can play basketball in the winter. You can play it in the summer. (too)

____

4 Rita is good at tennis. She's good at badminton. (too)

____

WRITING

A PREPARE Read the post below. What sport or activity should Janice try? Write notes. Use the steps in Exercise D to help you.

I am a 53-year-old woman. I'd like to try a sport or activity. I don't like team sports and I have problems with my back. Does anyone have any advice for me? What should I try? Thanks!

Janice

B Write your recommendation. Use *also*, *too* and *as well* to add information.

W— structuring emails

A Read the invitation. What is it for?

1 an anniversary **2** a birthday **3** a wedding

hosted by Ray and Marcia

May 15, 12:00 pm–6:00 pm

Old Creek Golf Club

20 Ocean Drive, Tampa, Florida, US

The ceremony will take place at 12 noon. After the ceremony, there will be a lunch at the Clubhouse, followed by a reception. Formal dress.

For more details, please contact our wedding planner, Kelly Olson: kelly@floridaweddings.nett

B Work in pairs. Read again and answer the questions.

1 Whose wedding is it?

2 When is the wedding?

3 Where is the wedding?

4 Who do you contact for more details?

C Read Justin's email to the wedding planner. Number the steps 1–6.

> Dear Ms. Olson,
>
> I am writing to ask you for some information.
>
> My wife and I are going to attend Ray and Marcia's wedding in Tampa on May 15. We would like to book a double room in a hotel nearby. Could you please recommend somewhere?
>
> Also, we are going to arrive at Tampa airport late at night. Is there public transportation at that time? Or should I take a taxi?
>
> I look forward to hearing from you.
>
> Kind regards,
>
> Justin Blake

___ Ask for a recommendation

___ Start a formal email with the title and the last name of the person you're writing to

___ Friendly phrase before the end of the email

___ Reason for writing

___ Ask about transportatioin

___ End a formal email with the full name of the writer

D Complete the email with the words in the box.

cost could dear information look regards writing

1 ________ Mr. Young,

I am 2 ________ to ask for some 3 ________ about a reception room in your hotel.

I am going to be 30 years old this year, and I want to have a big party to celebrate. I am going to invite around 150 people.

4 ________ you please tell me how much the room costs?

Also, could you tell me how much food would 5 ________ for the guests?

I 6 ________ forward to hearing from you.

Kind 7 ________,

Gemma Lai

Structuring emails

We usually write formal emails to people we don't know, often to ask for information.

We start formal emails with *Dear* + *Mr./Mrs./Ms.* + last name.

We often give a reason for writing and then ask some questions.

Before the end of the email, we use a friendly phrase (*I look forward to seeing / hearing from you.*)

You can end formal emails with any of these phrases: *Sincerely yours*, *Regards*, *Kind regards*. Then your full name.

We don't usually use contractions in formal emails.

I am writing to ask for information **NOT** *I'm writing to ask for information.*

WRITING

A PREPARE Read the invitation. What is it for?

Hosted by Sophie and Nadim August 6, 6:00 pm–10:00 pm

10 Jack McClure Place, Northbridge, New South Wales, Australia

Come and celebrate ten wonderful years together! We hope you can all come!

P.S. The Tired Traveler is a great small hotel nearby. Write to Mr. and Mrs. Foster for reservations.

B Write an email to *The Tired Traveler* hotel to make a reservation. Write about the following:

- What kind of room would you like?
- How long do you want the room for?
- When and how are you going to arrive?
- What else do you want to know?

C Work in pairs. Read each other's emails. Did your partner use formal language?

UNIT 7

Lesson 7.3, Listening, Exercise B
7.6 **C = Colleague E = Emma**

C: Hi, Emma. Did you have a good vacation?

E: Yeah! It was amazing, thank you!

C: Where did you go?

E: To China.

C: China? Wow! That's interesting. What did you do? Did you visit the Great Wall?

E: Yes, I did. It was … well, great! Do you want to see some photos?

C: Sure … So, why did you choose China?

E: Well, I didn't choose it, actually. I went on a 'mystery vacation'.

C: What do you mean, a 'mystery vacation'?

E: I used a company that organizes your vacation for you. But they don't tell you anything about it until you get to the airport.

C: Huh? So how did it work?

E: I told them about my interests, how long I wanted to go for, and my budget – I said I could spend about $1,500 – then they chose the hotels and activities … and basically created a vacation for me.

C: So, did you know your destination? Did you know the vacation was in China?

E: No, I didn't. I didn't know anything except the date and the airport. When I arrived at the check-in desk, I got a letter with the details. I found out that I was on a flight to Beijing. It was a complete surprise!

C: That's so cool! Was it cheap?

E: No, it wasn't. It was very expensive, actually. But they organized the flights, hotels, transportation, entertainment – they did everything!

C: So where did you stay?

E: In hotels, but I also stayed with a Chinese family in Shanghai. And I slept on a train, too – the overnight train to Shanghai.

C: Did the company organize that?

E: Yes, but I didn't know anything about it before. When I was in Beijing, I got an email about my next destination. Then in Shanghai, I got another email, and so on.

C: What else did you do?

E: I went sightseeing in Beijing, went on a boat trip on a river and climbed mountains in the forest.

C: Did you see any pandas?

E: Yes, I did. Hold on … Here's some pandas that I went to see in Chengdu.

C: Wow! I love pandas! You did so much. But why did you decide to do a mystery vacation?

E: Well, I wanted an adventure. Every day was a surprise and different. It felt new and exciting. And I didn't have to organize a thing!

C: It sounds great! I want to try a mystery vacation, too!

UNIT 8

Lesson 8.1, Listening, Exercise A
8.3 **M = Marta S = Stefan**

M: Stefan, what are you doing?

S: I'm looking for something to eat for dinner tonight, but we don't have anything I can eat.

M: What do you mean? There's lots of food in there. Why don't we have pizza?

S: Oh, no! No, no. I can't have pizza.

M: Why not? You love pizza.

S: I do, I do … but I'm on a diet and pizza is one of the things I can't eat.

M: Is this the diet in your magazine? I told you – you *don't* need to lose weight.

S: I know, but I want to. Anyway, it's a very healthy diet.

M: OK, so what *can* you eat then?

S: Oh, lots of things: beef, chicken, fish …

M: Vegetables?

S: Of course!

M: So why not pizza?

S: Oh, well I can't eat bread. So, no pizza. Now, what's in the fridge? Is there any chicken?

M: Uh … So, about the chicken …

S: Where is it? I'm sure we had some chicken …

M: There isn't any chicken. I … uh … ate it yesterday.

S: Oh, OK. Right. Well, I can eat vegetables. Now, what do we have … Oh, yes! We have some mushrooms, and some broccoli. Oh, and we have a carrot, too … That's good.

M: Mushrooms, broccoli and a carrot? We can't eat mushrooms, broccoli and a carrot for dinner! What else is there?

S: Uh … we might have some fruit … There's an orange! It's a little old, but it's OK. Hmm … we don't have any apples or bananas … we need to get some fruit next week …

M: We can't just eat fruit for dinner! I'm not sure about this diet. Why do we need to change? I think we have a healthy diet. We eat a lot of fresh food.

S: Hmm … Maybe …

M: … and we never eat unhealthy food like cake or chips.

S: Hmm … Yes, you're right! This diet is a terrible idea.

M: Great. So, let's make dinner. Pizza?

UNIT 9

Lesson 9.1, Listening, Exercise B
9.3 **S = Sophie J = Johan**

S: Hey, Johan.

J: Hey!

S: How are things? What are you doing?

J: I'm well, thanks. I'm having coffee at the café in the park.

S: Oh, I miss the café in the park. Is Tom there?

J: No, just me. Excuse me – espresso, please? Oh, sorry! How embarrassing! I just ordered a coffee from a customer. I thought he was a waiter – he's wearing a white shirt and a tie, and carrying some cups.

S: Oops! Is the park busy?

J: Yes, it's very busy. Ooh! There's a woman near me. I *think* she's a runner – she's wearing a t-shirt and sneakers. She's very angry. She's trying to get a bottle of water but no one is serving her.

S: Mm.

J: Oh, Sophie, you should see this – there's a tall man and a short woman coming this way. They're wearing *really* strange clothes. She's in pajamas!

S: What? They're in pajamas?

J: No, the *man* isn't wearing pajamas. He's dressed like a pirate! Haha! He's in a black jacket, a bandana and a hat with three corners.

S: Haha! That's odd! I wonder why they're dressed like that …

J: Hang on, I'll ask … Excuse me, why are you wearing those clothes? Oh, I see, thanks. Apparently, they're doing a charity run.

S: Oh, I see!

J: Aww! How cute …

S: What's happening now?

J: There's a little girl in a pretty pink party dress with a pink ribbon in her hair. She's holding her mother's hand. I think it's her first party. She looks very sweet!

S: Awww …

J: Anyway, tell me about you. What are you doing?

S: Well, it was really cold this morning, so …

Lesson 9.2, Listening, Exercise B

9.4 **A = Announcer**

A: Hello, shoppers and welcome to Greenfield Department Store. Would you like to win 1,000 dollars? Then enter our job swap competition! Swap your job for one day and you could win the money. To enter our job swap competition, go to the clothing department on level two, which is by the café. Make sure you enjoy some coffee and a sandwich while you're there! Registration opens this morning at ten o'clock and stays open until four o'clock this afternoon, so make sure you register your name and contact information today.

UNIT 10

Lesson 10.1, Listening, Exercise A

10.1 **P = Presenter C = Clarice Mk = Mark J = Janek Ma = Maria**

P: With us today is Clarice Steinburg, a location scout. Clarice worked on this year's top movie, *The Adventurer*, which won eight Oscars! Clarice, welcome! Tell us about your job. What does a location scout do?

C: Well, I find the best places to make a movie. I don't mean a studio; I mean actual locations, like a building, a city or a landscape.

P: I see, I see … Well, Clarice, we have a lot of questions for you tonight from people here in the audience. First up is Mark from London. What's your question, Mark?

Mk: Yes. Hi, Clarice. *The Adventurer* is a great movie, and the locations are amazing.

C: Thank you.

Mk: A lot of the story takes place on a beach in California. Which beach is it?

C: Well, we didn't actually film in California. We filmed the beach scenes in Mexico.

P: Mexico? Why was that?

C: It's very difficult to film in California because it's really crowded and there are people everywhere. Often, the beaches are busier than the city! It's difficult to close a busy beach for days to make a movie.

P: So, it was better to film in Mexico?

C: That's right. The beaches in Mexico are quieter than in California.

P: Was it expensive?

C: No. Actually, it was more expensive to film in the US than in Mexico. Even with the cost of flights and hotels, Mexico was cheaper than the US.

P: OK. We're ready for another question. Janek?

J: Thank you. The part in the desert is amazing. Is that Mexico, too?

C: No, we shot that bit in Morocco.

P: Wow! Why Morocco? That's so far from California!

C: Yes, Morocco is much farther than Mexico! But there are some old buildings in the part of the desert where we filmed, and the sand is very red, so it's more interesting.

P: Next question. Maria?

Ma: Hi, Clarice.

C: Hi!

Ma: I loved *The Adventurer*. The scenes in the jungle are really beautiful. Where did you film them? I want to go there!

C: I'm sorry. We filmed those right here in Los Angeles!

P: No! There aren't any jungles in L.A.!

C: I know! We created that location on a computer! It was all in a studio in downtown Los Angeles. It's very difficult to film in a real jungle.

Lesson 10.3, Listening, Exercise B

10.5 **G = Greg M = Marcus**

G: We're here with survival expert Marcus James to hear his advice on how to survive in the wild. Marcus, thank you for joining us.

M: You're welcome. Thanks for having me on the show.

G: So Marcus, if you're lost and you need to stay warm or cook some food, what's the best way to start a fire? Two pieces of dry wood?

M: Well, Greg, the easiest thing to do is to carry a box of matches or a lighter in your backpack, and use that to light a fire.

G: Oh, yes … I suppose so. So how about some other tips? For example, what are the safest plants to eat? How can I catch animals?

M: Again, 95 percent of hikers have energy bars in their backpack. They don't need 'macho survival techniques'. Always plan to take a few important things with you, like a pocketknife, a lantern and a phone. Then, you don't have to catch animals! And, did you know, Greg, you can actually survive for up to three weeks without food? And that's a fact!

G: Really? So, what about Chuck Adams? Is his advice wrong?

M: It's not bad – I just don't think it's the most useful advice. For example, if you want to stay dry, take a raincoat. You don't need to build anything.

G: What's the most useful advice in your opinion?

M: The best advice I can give you is to be prepared. When you decide to go hiking, tell someone where you're going. On the hike, check your map and compass. Take lots of photos on your phone. They can help you find your way back later. And if you get lost, leave signs so people can find you. For example, leave pieces of clothing on a tree. And remember to keep warm. The truth is, most people don't die because they get lost – they die because they don't prepare.

UNIT 11

Lesson 11.1, Listening, Exercise B

11.1 **B = Bianca E = Ella**

B: This article is called 'Look Good, Feel Good'. It has some nice clothes and some good health tips. You want a healthier lifestyle, don't you, Ella?

E: Mmm?

B: Actually, there are some really nice clothes in this article. What should I wear tonight? Those are nice pants. Should I wear pants tonight, Ella? Or a dress? I think I'll wear a dress. It's a party, after all.

E: Mmm.

B: Anyway, here's some good advice on how to take care of your body. Oh, you shouldn't spend too much time on your phone – the screen is bad for your eyes.

E: Mmm?

B: I like this one. Sleep is good for your heart. I think your heart is very healthy, Ella. You're always asleep! And sleeping on a firm bed helps with a bad back. Interesting.

E: Mmm?

B: And do you know how to improve your brain? You should listen to classical music every day.

E: Oh?

B: Yes! It says it here. Ha! I didn't know Mozart could make you more intelligent!

E: Mmm.

B: Ooh! Rolling a small ball under your foot is good for you. It helps the blood flow around your body.

E: Really?

B: You should eat yogurt to keep your stomach healthy. Everyone knows that! Coffee is good for you. Is it? Oh, I see. You should put it on your skin. It makes it soft.

E: Mmm.

B: But you shouldn't drink too much coffee – it keeps you awake. Ella? Coffee keeps you awake. Ella? Are you awake?

E: Mmm? Oh, yes, please.

B: What do you mean 'yes, please'? Are you listening to me?

E: Of course I am. You just offered me some cake.

B: I said 'awake'. You never listen to me. I'm giving you all of this great health advice for free and as usual, you're *not listening*!

E: Mmhmm. Sorry, what did you say?

UNIT 12

Lesson 12.1, Listening, Exercise B

12.1 **J = Juliet M = Mario K = Kelly**

J: Guys! I'm so sorry I'm late. I needed to finish some things at work.

M: It's Saturday, Juliet. Why are you working on the weekend?

J: Oh, things are really busy at the moment. It's terrible. I'm at work all day, then I have to leave at five to pick up the children. Then in the evenings, I'm always busy with them. Well, actually, I'm usually in the car because I have to take them to their dance classes, or soccer, or swimming.

M: I read an article in the *Guardian* about time management. It had some useful tips.

K: Yeah, I saw that, too.

J: Well, I need some tips. Something has to change. Tomorrow, I'm going to make a long list of everything I need to do.

M: No, don't make long lists!

J: Why not?

M: Because you can't finish everything. The article said you have to make a list of five things.

J: Only five?

M: That's right. But I never make lists. What's the point?

K: I like making long lists because that way I remember everything. But maybe I should try the five-list idea.

J: I make lists, too, but I'm going to try that idea at work next week. My biggest problem is that I can't say no, so I have too much to do.

M: I'm like that, too. I agreed to work full time this week, but then I'm studying for my degree in the evening. I need to finish an essay. It's due in on Monday, but there just aren't enough hours in the day. I don't know what I'm going to do.

K: Are you going to finish your essay this weekend?

M: I think I can find time to plan it tonight, but I'm definitely not going to finish it. It's difficult to study when I'm tired.

K: You need to understand your body clock. When do you work best? I'm definitely a morning person.

M: Yes, I think I am, too.

J: Maybe you should ask your boss if you can work in the evenings, so you can study in the mornings?

M: That's a great idea! I'm going to see him tomorrow, so I can ask him then.

K: Or maybe you could take a day off? It's impossible to do everything, so don't worry about it!

M: But you're really organized, Kelly. I'm not! I find it hard to prioritize.

K: Just make a list, then decide which are the most important things.

M: Why make a list when everything is a priority. I can't decide what's most important, so I do nothing!

J: I know just what you mean!

12.9 Lesson 12.3, Listening, Exercise B
N = Narrator S = Shani L = Luke W = Wai J = Jean M = Maria

N: Shani Zahra

S: I use Facebook for news about friends and family and sometimes Twitter, to see what's trending, but I don't post much. I studied business at a university and now I work for a large bank so my number one social network is LinkedIn. I like to see what's happening in the business world. I blog about business and one day I'd love to teach it.

N: Luke Fox

L: I connect with friends on Instagram – or face to face at our local café. I follow loads of people on Twitter. I love it! A friend of mine is an actor and he tweets about the acting world and the theater. He's so funny! And I follow the latest news stories. I teach 8-year-old children and they know all the news. I might sign up to Snapchat so I can keep up-to-date!

N: Wai Zhu

W: I don't mind Facebook, but I much prefer Instagram. I like taking pictures and Instagram is a great place to share them. I also use WeChat a lot. It's really popular back home in China, so I use it to keep in touch with my friends and family. A lot of the people at work also use LinkedIn, so I might set up an account, too. I don't want to miss out!

N: Jean Walker

J: I only use Facebook. Sometimes I use it to catch up with my five friends, but usually it's to see my family. I have four children and six grandchildren. They put photos on Facebook and I get to see what they're doing. Sometimes I 'like' a photo, but I can't do much more than that, I'm afraid. I might try some other social media networks, but at the moment I don't really know how to use them.

N: Maria Ricci

M: I check Facebook every two hours. It's a great way to keep in touch with old school friends you haven't seen for ten years. However, for photos, I like Snapchat best because pictures only stay online for ten seconds after I send them.

Macmillan Education Limited
4 Crinan Street
London N1 9XW

Companies and representatives throughout the world

American Language Hub Level 1B Student's Book ISBN 978-1-380-04693-2
American Language Hub Level 1B Student's Book with Student's App
ISBN 978-1-380-04687-1

Text, design and illustration © Macmillan Education Limited 2020
Written by Peter Maggs and Catherine Smith

With thanks to Edward Price and Carol Goodwright for additional authoring and to Signature Manuscripts for the Grammar Hub pages.

The authors have asserted their right to be identified as the authors of this work in accordance with the Copyright, Designs and Patents Act 1988.

The right of Sue Kay and Vaughan Jones to be identified as authors of the Speaking Pages in this work has been asserted by them in accordance with the Copyright, Designs and Patents Act 1988.

First published 2020

All rights reserved. No part of this publication may be reproduced, stored in a retrieval system, or transmitted in any form or by any means, electronic, mechanical, photocopying, recording, or otherwise, without the prior written permission of the publishers.

Designed by emc design ltd
Illustrated by Rasmus Juul, Rose Frith represented by Lemonade Illustration Agency, Peter Lubach (Beehive illustration)
Cover design by Restless
Cover image by Plainpicture/Cultura/dotdotred
Picture research by Emily Taylor
Café Hub videos produced by Creative Listening
Café Hub video scripts written by James and Luke Vyner

The authors and publishers would like to thank the following for permission to reproduce their photographs:

Alamy Andor Bujdoso p117(tr), Danita Delimont p96(br), EyeEm pXXVIII(4), Hero Images pp86, p114(2) Lebrecht Music and Arts Photo Library p65(b), David Pearson pXX(3), Stefano Politi Markovina pXX(7), Andrej Sokolow/dpa pXX(tcr); **BrandX** pXX(6,11); **Corbis** pXXIX(4); **Getty Images** pXVIII(2), XVIII(5), XIX(2,5,8,10,11,13), XX(1,5,8,9), XXII(6,7,8,9), TK XXIII-XXV (2.2.1, 2.2.5, 2.2.6), XXVI(Chichen Itza), 4kodiak p77, Mireya Acierto p107(2), Tony Anderson pXX(10), Sally Anscombe p114(tm), ArabianEye p94(cr), Petri Artturi Asikainen p82(1,2), Gregory Bajor pXVIII(3), Barcroft Media p114(1), Thomas Barwick pXXX(tl, tm), XXXI(tl), David M. Benett pXX(tr), benimage pXXIX(5), Bettmann Archive p65(d,e), Blend Images pp66(br), 82(3), XX(4), XXVIII(3), Gary Burchell p113, Peter Burnett p106, Caiaimage p87, Ramsey Cardy pXXV, Steve Chenn pXXII(1), Creative Crop pXIX(15), Corbis pp61, 63(3), 65(a), Cultura pp74(bl), 96(chuck), 104(tcr), XXX(caitlin), XXXI(br), Jake Curtis p83(b), Digital Vision p78-79, 90(tr), 91, Zach Dischner pXXVI(wind surfing), Nick Dolding p95, Dorling Kindersley p89(boots, jacket), 99(gifts), E+ p93, XXII(10), Johannes Eisele p111, Andrew Errington pXXII(5), EyeEm p66(bm), 67(br), 68-69(background), 90(tl), 101, 117(tl), fStop p108-109(background), Mitchell Funk p62(2), Jamie Garbutt p114(tr), Geber86 pp84(3), 107(1), 112, XXII(3), Gilaxia p118-119(crowd), Sylvain Grandadam p102-103, HannamariaH pXXI(1-4), Daniel Hernanz Ramos p63(6), Hero Images pp67(Kate956), 85(tl), Neil Holmes pp70(2), XVIII(9), Howardkingsnorth p63(5), Image Source pp85(cl), XXII(4), IndiaPictures p62(1), Interim Archives p64, iStockphoto pp89(dress, suit), XIX(3, 14), XX(2), XXIX(1), XXVII, Maya Karkalicheva pXXX(marta), Howard Kingsnorth p92(bl), Glyn Kirk p83(a), kulicki p118-119(background), Andrew Lipovsky p67(LisaChorley), Lonely Planet Images pp66(t), 94(tl), 117(tm), Lorado p104(t), Martin-dm p66(girl with backpack), Dean Mitchell pXX(12), Moment pp65(c), Moment pXVIII(12), Mytruestory Photography p67(bl), National Geographic pXXVI(restaurant), National Geographic Magazines p74(tl), Ed Norton p67(tl), Numbeos p108(bl), Ourtneyk p71, PeopleImages pXXX(tr), PongMoji p84(1), Portra ehf p104(bcl, br), Portland Press Herald p81, PYMCA pp70(3), XVIII(11), José Reis Jr p92(bcl), Lilly Roadstones pp117(bm), XXX(Luis), Robert Harding World Imagery p94(bl), XXII(12), Tim Robberts pp67(TravelBob), p114(3), Kirill Rudenko p82(4), Michael Schwalbe pXVIII(4), Pascal Le Segretain pXX(cr), Nick Sinclair pXXVIII(1), Alexander Spatari p68-69(b), StockFood pXIX(6), Phillip Suddick p107(3), Fredrik Telleus pXXX(martin), Alys Tomlinson p52(6), Universal Images Group Betsie van der Meer ppXXII(11), XXVIII(2), Vetta p84(2), Westend61 pp96(tr), XXI(bl), James Whitaker p85(bl), WIN-Initiative pXVIII(6), xijian p117(bl), Zeigler p72-73; **Hinterhaus** Productions p100(tl); **ImageSource** pXIX(1); **iStockphoto** pp100(bl), 105; **Photodisc** pp98-99(background), XXIX(3); **Shutterstock** Hartmut Albert p92(tcl), Africa Studio p88-89, Andrmoel pXXVI(b), Elenovsky p89(shirt), Angelo Gilardelli p89(hat), Jag_cz pXVIII(10), Art Konovalov pp70(4), XVIII(14), Teddy Leung pXVIII(1), Elijah Lovkoff pXVIII(13), Milanzeremski p74(cr), S/Mimo p89(scarf), Mishu88 pXVIII(8), Filip Olejowski p89(coat), Pavel L Photo and Video p63(4), Photka pXXIX(1), Steve Photography p92(tl), Sova Vitalij pXXII(2); **Stockbyte** pXXIX(2) Stockbyte/PunchStock pp70(1), XVIII(7); **Thinkstock** pp89(jumper), XIX(4,7,9,12), XXIX(1).

Commissioned photographs in the Café Hubs by Creative Listening.

These materials may contain links for third party websites. We have no control over, and are not responsible for, the contents of such third party websites. Please use care when accessing them.

The inclusion of any specific companies, commercial products, trade names or otherwise, does not constitute or imply its endorsement or recommendation by Macmillan Education Limited.

Printed and bound in Uruguay

2023

5